Leninism: a sociological interpretation

Themes in the Social Sciences

Editors: Jack Goody & Geoffrey Hawthorn

The aim of this series is to publish books which will focus on topics of general and interdisciplinary interest in the social sciences. They will be concerned with non-European cultures and with developing countries, as well as with industrial societies. The emphasis will be on comparative sociology and, initially, on sociological, anthropological and demographic topics. These books are intended for undergraduate teaching, but not as basic introductions to the subjects they cover. Authors have been asked to write on central aspects of current interest which have a wide appeal to teachers and research students, as well as to undergraduates.

Other books in the series

Edmund Leach: *Culture and Communication: the logic by which symbols are connected: an introduction to the use of structuralist analysis in social anthropology*

Anthony Heath: *Rational Choice and Social Exchange: a critique of exchange theory*

P. Abrams and A. McCulloch: *Communes, Sociology and Society*

Jack Goody: *The Domestication of the Savage Mind*

Jean-Louis Flandrin: *Families in Former Times: kinship, household and sexuality*

John Dunn: *Western Political Theory in the Face of the Future*

David Thomas: *Naturalism and Social Science: a post-empiricist philosophy of social science*

Claude Meillassoux: *Maidens, Meal and Money: capitalism and the domestic community*

Leninism:
a sociological interpretation

DAVID LANE

University of Birmingham

CAMBRIDGE UNIVERSITY PRESS

Cambridge
London   New York   New Rochelle
Melbourne   Sydney

Published by the Press Syndicate of the University of Cambridge
The Pitt Building, Trumpington Street, Cambridge CB2 1RP
32 East 57th Street, New York, NY 10022, USA
296 Beaconsfield Parade, Middle Park, Melbourne 3206, Australia

First published 1981

Printed and bound in Great Britain by
Redwood Burn Limited
Trowbridge & Esher

British Library Cataloguing in Publication Data
Lane, David
Leninism. – (Themes in the social sciences).
1. Communism
I. Title   II. Series
335.43   HX40   80–41533
ISBN 0 521 23855 2 hard covers
ISBN 0 521 28259 4 paperback

Contents

Contents

Figures

Preface

The Bolshevik Revolution of October 1917 heralded what has become the major social and political transformation of the twentieth century. Despite its failures, and its horrors, it is widely recognised as providing a model for the transition from capitalism (or pre-capitalism) to communism (or various forms of socialism). This book is addressed to analysing some of the theoretical presuppositions of Bolshevism: the ideas about revolution held by Lenin and their transformation into an ideology of Leninism after his death. It considers the impact on Russia of the political seizure of power by the Bolsheviks in 1917: but it is not a book about history – it deals with some of the major interpretations or explanations of the Revolution in Russia. The first chapters outline Lenin's approach to Marxism and consider those elements of his views which might be considered to be at the core of his theory of revolution. Studied thematically, the various parts of his thinking are shown to be complementary in providing an analysis of capitalism and the justification for socialist revolution. These chapters are not exhaustive: they do not consider in depth Lenin's views on many topics and they focus on his analysis of capitalist society rather than on his philosophy. It is believed that a relatively short, concise but not unsympathetic account of Lenin's thinking on revolution fulfils a current need, when so many books deal either with specialist aspects of his thought or (all too often) regard Lenin as a conspiratorial actor rather than as a thinker.

The objective of the first two chapters is to show how Lenin's ideas (and those of his fellow-revolutionaries) were conditioned by the environment of Russia at that time and the implications of this for political activity. In Chapter 1, an attempt is made to uncover the ideological and theoretical foundations of Lenin's approach to society. In Chapter 2, the major components of Lenin's theory of revolution are outlined and are set against the cultural heritage and changing economic structure of Tsarist Russia. Thirdly, we focus on the Bolsheviks in power. Attention is given to the process of revolution: what features of society continue into the supposedly new epoch and how do the forces for change retain their vigour? In this context, Stalinism is defined and considered from four contrasting viewpoints: Marxist–Leninist, transitional society, totalitarianism and cultural continuity. Here again the preconditions given by Russian culture and the impact of the ideology of Leninism, derived from Lenin's own writings, are emphasised. An attempt is made to provide a detached analysis of Stalin's policies by separating the theoretically sustained explanations from the denunciatory attacks. In pointing to some of the subsequent problems of the October Revolution, I have tried not to succumb to the current 'masked intellectual terrorism' (to use the words of Pierre Vilar) or the 'moral blackmail' (E. H. Carr) which pervades our intellectual culture in relation to Soviet society (quotations cited by Corrigan, Ramsay and Sayer 1979: 6).

After considering the strengths and weaknesses of the various explanations, an attempt is made to generalise about the revolutionary process. Here the theories of Talcott Parsons and Karl Marx are seen to be complementary in many ways, and it is suggested that these two theoretical approaches may be synthesised to account for the happenings in Russia and a model of the revolutionary process is suggested. Finally, the limitations of Bolshevism as an approach to conditions pertaining in contemporary Western Europe are outlined. Comparison of present-day Western Europe and its problems (systemic though they may be) with Lenin's Russia show 'Leninism' as politics to be no longer appropriate to the problems of Western European socialist reconstruction – though its relevance to underdeveloped countries is another matter.

The approach of the book is not one of Talmudic exegesis concerned with textual analysis of items of Lenin's writings. Nor is it an attempt to 'prescribe' correct contemporary policy on some issue in terms of what Lenin said. At the same time this book does provide an interpretation of Lenin's ideas (and the role of ideas as ideologies) which has implications for the analysis of modern societies. The aim of the book is to provide an account of Lenin's method, of the interconnectedness of his ideas and of their relevance to the problems which confronted the socialist movement of his time in Russia. In so far as policy is concerned, my first aim is to uncover a Leninist approach to politics and society. Lenin's strength as a political activist lies in his method: the combination of serious Marxist sociological analysis and political tactics, and this is considered in contrast with the methods of non-Marxists. My interest in Lenin lies more in his political and economic analysis of the unfolding of Russian and world capitalism than in his more philosophical ideas. I have, therefore, attempted briefly to outline Lenin's methodological assumptions and to express in more detail his social analysis. My task is to point out that Lenin's work is historically specific, in so far as his tactics and politics are concerned, and that to tear out particular parts from the whole is illegitimate. From my own standpoint, much of the present literature which discusses Lenin is not so much incorrect, or based on an inadequate reading of Lenin, as it is inappropriate when applied to the world of Western Europe in the last quarter of the twentieth century. I have attempted to appraise the impact of revolution in Russia and to set Lenin's ideas against the happenings in the post-revolutionary period.

There are then four distinct, though related, topics: Lenin's analysis of revolution; Leninism as an ideology legitimating the Russian Revolution; a detached analysis of revolution, and the relevance today of Lenin and the Russian Revolution. This is an ambitious agenda and these are controversial questions. There is a clear danger that covering such a wide canvas will lead to superficiality and unevenness in the coverage of alternative positions. But I believe that a synoptic account of Lenin's ideas, the Russian Revolution and the sociology of revolution, in a relatively short book, will enable us to see these questions in a somewhat different light than hitherto. The book then does not set out to rival the more comprehensive works on these topics, neither can it attempt to cover in detail alternative views – these I have summarised to bring out their inadequacies in the light of my own approach. The work does not purport to be a history of Lenin's thought or of its interconnectedness with world history. Topics are considered *thematically* not historically. The book is intended for different constituencies: for historians, political scientists and sociologists who require a short and succinct analysis of Lenin's views on revolution, and an exposition of some of the more important interpretations of Stalinism, and it may also be of interest to those concerned with the theories and the process of social change.

I have followed the scientific citations practice of name of author followed by date of publication and, where relevant, page (e.g. Smith 1979: 241). For the works of Marx, Engels, and Lenin, I have amended this somewhat to indicate the brief title of the work or article, e.g. Engels, *Ludwig Feuerbach*, 1951. I have referred to the pagination of the three-volume edition of Lenin's *Selected Works* (SW), 1977 edition, or to the *Collected Works* (CW), 1960–70 edition. (Note that there are various editions of the three-volume *Selected Works*, whose pagination and

English translation are not consistent.) A complete list of articles or works cited by Lenin is to be found in the bibliography.

Many acknowledgements in a book of this kind are in order. I would like to thank Geoffrey Hawthorn, David Held and two anonymous referees for many comments and suggestions on earlier drafts. Cathy Marsh also saved me from making some mistakes.

March 1980

Lenin's approach to Marxism

In the West, non-Marxist writers have regarded Lenin's thought as contributing very little to political and sociological theory. Most Western writers on Lenin have seen him first as a revolutionary activist rather than as a social theorist. Conquest, for instance, says that 'the power and influence of [Lenin's] writing has arisen largely from the fact that the author himself carried out a major revolution' (Conquest 1972: 12). Carew Hunt writes that 'The theoretical side of Lenin is in a sense not serious. It is in the sure instinct with which he grasps the reality of a given situation that his genius lies, though the tactics then adopted are always justified with Marxist texts' (Carew Hunt 1963: 171). Sartre has dismissed Lenin's philosophy as 'unthinkable' and Merleau-Ponty has described it as 'expedient' (cited by Althusser 1971: 33).

Kolakowski (1978: vol. 2) is the latest and most sophisticated of this school: 'To Lenin . . . all theoretical questions were merely instruments of a single aim, the revolution; and the meaning of all human affairs, ideas, institutions and values resided exclusively in their bearing in the class struggle. . . . [B]y a natural progression, the dictatorship first exercised over society in the name of the working class and then over the working class in the name of the party, was now applied to the party itself, creating the basis for a one-man tyranny' (pp. 383, 489). Such writers tend to conflate Lenin's thought, the legitimating doctrine of Leninism devised in the USSR after Lenin's death and the practices of Stalin: these different phenomena are conveniently labelled by such writers as 'Leninism'.

One reason for this neglect of Lenin as a theorist is that, as Meyer has pointed out, his views are 'based on a philosophy that is uncongenial to thinkers in our culture' (Meyer 1957: 1; see also Althusser 1971: 37). The *weltanschauung* of liberal-democracy is so strongly held by many of Lenin's Western critics that they are unable to penetrate his tactical policies to comprehend the emancipatory qualities and creative aspects of his thought. But not all Western non-Marxist commentators have made such a negative evaluation: of particular note are Meyer (1957) and Harding (1977 and 1980), who have both sought to provide a cogent summary and a more sympathetic interpretation of Lenin's theory and practice.

Marxists have been even more divided about Lenin. Most Western Marxists have had little time for Lenin and attention has, at least until the late 1970s, been focussed on the young Marx (Anderson 1976; see below p. 89). Lukacs, as early as 1924, is exceptional in describing Lenin as 'the greatest thinker to have been produced by the revolutionary working-class movement since Marx' (Lukacs 1970: 9). But it was only in the 1970s that many serious Western Marxists turned to consider Lenin's ideas: in particular Timpanaro (1975), Hoffman (1975), Claudin-Urondo (1977), Althusser (1971), Liebman (1975) and Corrigan, Ramsay and Sayer (1978). In the Communist world, however, Lenin is held in high esteem as philosopher, sociologist and revolutionary politician (see, for example, Stalin 1934a; Mao Tse-Tung 1964).

But here again Lenin has been the subject of abuse from many communists and ex-communists alike who have considered Lenin's thought, or the doctrine of Leninism, to be an unacceptable development or extension of Marxist thought. This has a long history going back before the Revolution with criticisms by Luxemburg (1961). Also, and perhaps of more importance, is the fact that the seizure of power by the Bolsheviks in 1917 linked Lenin's theories with the practice of the Soviet Union and provided a catalyst for the principled opposition of many Marxists to Lenin's version of Marxism: Pannekoek (1975) and Korsch (1970) are examples of this tendency which is echoed by the writers associated with *Telos* (see Santamaria and Manville 1976; Piccone 1977).

Yet a third group of Marxists considers Lenin to have developed Marxism and to have related it to the conditions of the twentieth century (Trotsky, see particularly 'The 21st Anniversary', 1970: 172–3; Garaudy 1970). At the same time, however, they have argued that a distinct break occurred between the theories of Marx and Lenin and the ideology of Marxism–Leninism as articulated by the Soviet Communist Party under Stalin and his successors.* These criticisms have to be related to the politics of the twentieth century, particularly the rise of the USSR as a world power and the problem this has subsequently created for European Communist parties and their Marxist critics.

---

* On different meanings of 'Leninism' and differences between Lenin and Stalin, see Gerratana (1977).

Introduction

In this book we shall be concerned with some of the divisions which have occurred within the framework of Marxist thought about Lenin's theories and their development. Some writers in their opposition to Lenin and the kind of Marxism he has developed have gone back to Marx's work to find the original source of Lenin's heresy; one important school has tried to develop a more humanistic type of Marxism, derived often from the work of the young Marx, and this is particularly in opposition to the writing of Engels (see P. Anderson 1976, Avineri 1968). There is thus a distinction made between Marx's thought and Marxism, and one which might be made in my view between Lenin's thought and Leninism. Ideas from the original writings are reinterpreted to gain an affinity with the interests (material or ideal) of political elites (or even counter elites). It seems to be true that unless ideas do gain this affinity, they are abandoned by political actors and become mere objects of intellectual thought and are only studied for their intrinsic interest. One way that they can be used, and which is quite foreign to their original intention, is to legitimate the activity of a ruling stratum, group or class. The process of elective affinity, to use a Weberian term (Gerth and Mills 1948: 62), applies to Communist parties' interpretation of Marx's and Lenin's thought as it does to various Christian churches' interpretations of the teaching of Christ.

This analogy, however, cannot be carried too far. For Marxism and Leninism, unlike Christianity, claim to be scientific theories to interpret and to change society. Hence they were devised first and foremost as a method of analysis and any particular 'teachings' have only a limited application; they become redundant and useless knowledge in the face of historical change. Marx*ism* and Lenin*ism* are the application and development of Marx's and Lenin's theories: it is quite un-Marxist to resolve an argument solely in terms of what Marx (or Lenin) said, unless related to its social context. Hence one cannot naively dichotomise Lenin's thought and Leninism, or Marx's thought and Marxism – though to be sure, there is an important difference between them. Social thought does not stay still but reflects, and changes with, new circumstances and problems; unless it is analysed as a movement in relation to a changing society it becomes merely a collection of museum pieces – one moves from an 'account' of Marx to Engels to Lenin as one would view different fossils in museum display cabinets. Leninism we may define as a set of values, beliefs and practices derived from the thought of Lenin and which are said to guide the actions of the leaders of Communist parties (whether in power or not). As such, it is much more than

3

the sum of Lenin's thoughts: it is an approach to politics and society. In this sense, Stalin described Leninism as 'Marxism in the era of imperialism and of the proletarian revolution . . . Leninism is the theory and tactics of the dictatorship of the proletariat in particular' (Stalin 1934a: 10).

Citing Stalin in this way immediately and directly confronts one with the fact that Marxism–Leninism is now a legitimating ideology of the world's ruling Communist parties and their sympathisers. But Marxism–Leninism is more than just that: it purports to provide an explanation and a course of political action to change the world, to introduce socialism. It is in this context that we shall examine it. But I shall not argue that Stalin was correct in saying that the policies he evolved in Russia, despite their affinity with Lenin, were appropriate to the development of socialism on a world scale. Rather, I shall attempt to show how Lenin's thought and policy (and Stalin's too) were closely related to conditions of Russia and of the world in the early twentieth century. As Lenin would concede, his prognostications and policies are time- and place-bound, and should not be confused with his method of analysis. Delineating the specific Russian and Soviet policies from his general method of analysis will lead to the clarification of the relevance of his work today.

What then are the methodological underpinnings to Lenin's thought, and what kinds of criticisms can one make of them? Here I do not intend to discuss in detail Lenin's philosophy of history or his methodology. The importance of Bolshevism lies in its social and political analysis – and it is only indirectly that method and philosophy become relevant. Most Western commentaries on Lenin pay little attention to his methodology and philosophy. Neither Harding nor Meyer systematically deals with these topics and the latter comments that the 'impact of philosophical beliefs and attitudes on policy in the Leninist movement and the Soviet State has been of no more than marginal importance' (Meyer 1957: 5). Lenin himself, however, as Meyer concedes, thought that dialectical materialism was the key to 'a correct understanding of reality and . . . expedient action' (*ibid.*: 8).

We might identify three assumptions derived from Marxism which inform Lenin's approach. Firstly, and strongly influenced by Engels, he emphasises a materialist position: this involves the priority of matter over mind, and the conditioning effects which nature exercises over man. The relationship of man and nature is a 'dialectical' one, there is an exchange between man and nature, man is limited by, yet he actively shapes, the physical and social world. Secondly, Lenin's analysis of society is predicated on an historical materialist viewpoint that history progresses through definite stages and that there is a replacement of capitalism by communism: this movement, however, can only be the result of activity by class conscious actors (individuals and collectivities). Thirdly, the interpretation of social facts has a class character and Marxists in the era of capitalism orientate their work to speed the rise of a communist society. Politics, sociology and history are sciences in the sense that they take account of the objective laws of nature which condition the evolution of society but, at the same time, Marxist writers attempt to influence the rate and direction of change. Freedom to act is the recognition of necessity: political class interests are inextricably part of human action; not only do they condition it, but they too are stimuli to action. A key to Lenin's approach to society is to recognise not only a political commitment to social change but also that an understanding of the world is necessary prior to changing it.

Leaving aside Lenin's actual political activity and its political conjuncture, how can one characterise the object and methods of his thought? All Lenin's work must be seen as being predicated on his analysis of the conditions for, and on the tactics of, the proletarian revolution: this was his major aim and his life work. (The Revolution is here considered to continue into the post-1917 period of the dictatorship of the proletariat in the Soviet Union.) Marx might be regarded as formulating laws of history while Lenin concentrated on political action – though he himself amended Marx's laws in the process. Lenin added a dimension of the theory of political *action* to Marxism. In addition to his methodology, there are three substantive components to Lenin's interpretation of capitalism. These three elements should be seen in combination and as such they may be regarded as Lenin's theory of socialist revolution. There is first, based on Marxist laws of historical materialism, the idea of the uneven development of capitalism; second, an organisational theory of decision-making and participation, to be utilised by the Party of the working class, and a policy of political action in relation to the state; and third, a theory of imperialism which describes the stage of capitalism in the early twentieth century (i.e. up to the First World War) and which focusses on the relations between the advanced capitalist states and those in the process of capitalist development. Each of these components was developed by Lenin on its own and one does not find in Lenin's works an analysis synthesising these components, and many commentators have tended to view each part on its own. It is important to stress that they are interconnected and that emphasis on one to the exclusion of another destroys the unity of Lenin's praxis. As Lenin points out many times, the Marxist approach is to see the whole and to consider the parts in relation to the whole. In addition to his analysis of capitalism, Lenin made a number of prognostications about socialism as an ideal state and provided what was in effect a theory of development for Soviet Russia after the Revolution. These substantive topics will be the concern of following chapters.

HISTORICAL AND DIALECTICAL MATERIALISM

Lenin's analysis of society is based on three inter-related foundations: materialism, dialectics, history. As a materialist, Lenin shares a general approach in common with Marx, and particularly Engels, as well as many other bourgeois scientists and writers such as Priestley and Feuerbach. The rise of natural science and the positivistic, agnostic and materialist world view accompanying it, was a concomitant of the rise of industrial capitalism. Lenin followed Engels in accepting materialism in the following terms: 'The great basic question of all philosophy, especially modern philosophy, is that concerning the relation of thinking and being. . . . Those who asserted the primacy of the spirit to nature and, therefore, in the last instance, assumed world-creation in some form or other . . . comprised of the camp of idealism. The others, who regarded nature as primary, belong to the various schools of materialism' (Engels, *Ludwig Feuerbach*, 1951: 334–5; see also Lenin, *Karl Marx, SW* 1: 20–1). Materialism, then, posits the priority of nature over mind. In the sense of diachronic priority we have the order: earth, life, man; or physical level, biological level, socio-economic level (see discussion in Timpanaro 1975: 34). Nature, which has its own laws independent of man, conditions him and it imposes constraints on him. This helps to explain why 'freedom' becomes the recognition, or the appreciation, of necessity. Lenin quotes Engels as pointing out that only bourgeois 'freedom' conceives of human action independently of natural laws; but in fact freedom consists of 'the knowledge of these laws, and in the possibility this gives to systematically making them work towards definite ends' (*Materialism and Empirio-Criticism, CW* 14: 187). 'The necessity of nature is primary, and human will and mind secondary' (*ibid.*: 188).

Materialism as a *weltanschauung* developed independently of Marxist thought. Positivism, and in Lenin's time, empirio-criticism and pragmatism, provided a materialist methodology for many natural scientists. Lenin went to some length to show that these doctrines could not be squared with Marxism and that scientists supporting this position tend to lapse into idealism. Although laws are discovered by men, their agnosticism leads them to believe that laws are made by men, rather than being independent of them in nature.

Lenin is also, we should note, very much at odds with today's 'radical' or 'critical' sociologists, such as Gouldner and Atkinson, who see the sociologist as actively 'intervening' in 'his subject matter. . . . His theories affect social attitudes and social life' (Atkinson 1972: 270). Gouldner regards the view that the laws of the social world are 'mirrored' in the sociologist's work as being 'a myth'; and he conceives of the social world as being 'conceptually constituted by the sociologist's cognitive commitments and all his other interests' (Gouldner 1971: 496). For Atkinson, the recognition of laws of nature makes Marxism a 'conservative force' (Atkinson 1972: 283) restricting the individual's creative activity. Similarly, Gouldner sees the 'liberating effects of the scientific revolution' as being a constraint on man and having been superseded by history (Gouldner 1971: 500). For Gouldner, 'Reflexive Sociology' is not distinguished by its subject matter, but by the relationship of the sociologist to his work (*ibid*.: 495). Lenin, on the other hand, sees purposeful social activity to be qualified by objective laws which are external to the individual actor. Lenin also emphasises that Marxist materialism is both dialectical and historical.

Dialectics is a most complex and wide-ranging topic which cannot be adequately covered here. My task is to describe Lenin's use of the dialectic as a method of analysis. One current interpretation of Lenin defines dialectical thought as the study of things in their relations and in process of development and change (Shirokov: 9). Dialectics is a method of thought which regards phenomena in nature as being in constant change and movement; change is a result of the contradictions, or the interaction of opposed forces, in nature.* Lenin explicitly saw that a dia-

---

* Stalin (1973: 302–5) defines four component parts of Marxist dialectical method. In summary these are: (1) That the phenomena of nature are inter-related to each other; any given phenomenon must be related and connected to its surrounding environment, in its interaction with other facts. (2) That nature is in a state of perpetual movement and change, dialectics considers the ways that nature is changing. Dialectics, says Engels, 'Takes things and their perceptual images essentially in their interconnexion, in their concatenation, in their movement, in their rise and disappearance' (*Dialectics of Nature*). Dialectical thinking is empirical: 'whatever facts emerge in experience must be recognised' (Shirokov: 11). (3) That development and change take place quantitatively and qualitatively, the former occurring gradually but leading to rapid

lectical approach meant that matter contains its own contradiction. 'Dialectics is the theory of knowledge of [Hegel and] Marxism. . . . The cognition of the contradictory parts [of a single whole] . . . is the essence of dialectics' (*On the Question of Dialectics*, *CW* 38: 362, 359). Hence dialectics is inevitably concerned with change. Class struggle is the social dialectic expressed in the laws of historical materialism which shows history to be moving through different stages: feudalism, capitalism, communism. A cornerstone of Lenin's historical analysis is the dialectical movement of history and the solution to the problem of this progression as it applied to Russia was to be found in the theory of combined or uneven development. Lenin's dialectics, in contrast to much philosophising, called for concreteness, for an empirical frame of reference. It seems clear that Lenin adopted, in his philosophical writings, a dialectical as well as a materialist approach, Corrigan *et al.* (1978: 37) argue that dialectics only appeared in Lenin's thought after 1914–16. A study of *Materialism* seems to me to show that this is false (see *CW* 38: 308, 329, where Lenin emphasises the dialectic).

A distinction made between materialism generally and the materialist theories of Marx and Engels is that the latter are applied to the evolution and structure of human societies. Materialism is grounded in the natural sciences, whereas *historical* materialism applies the dialectical and materialist method to the analysis of societies: from this position historical materialism is the science of society. Materialists observe, and consider themselves to be discovering, laws of the world of nature, whereas historical materialists see man as being conditioned by, and reacting upon, the world of nature. The specific application of historical materialism to societal analysis is a controversial topic among Marxists. There is general agreement that development of society occurs through the dialectical process of class struggle. The 'anatomy' of society is viewed through the prism of basis and superstructure: but the relative weights and importance of basis and superstructure respectively are matters of debate. This reflects a lack of consistency in Marx himself: in his early work (up to *The German Ideology*) Marx was less of a materialist than in his later work; and he tended to bring out the active role of man's intellect and moral personality in shaping nature. In Marx's later work (*Capital*) and in the writings of Engels, 'economic materialism', as a

and abrupt changes of state. (4) That contradictions are inherent in all phenomena of nature and development is a struggle of these opposing tendencies. 'Dialectics is the study of the contradiction *within the very essence of things* . . . it is the "struggle" of opposites' (Lenin, cited by Stalin 1973: 305).

primary influence in shaping man's environment, becomes clearer. It is this 'version' of Marxism that was adopted by Lenin and his compatriot Plekhanov, and has become an important component of Bolshevism. Indeed, Plekhanov's *Development of the Monist View of History* has been said to argue the 'determining influence of the economic substructure of society more fully even than Marx had attempted' (Harding 1977: 79).

Whatever contemporary Marxists may argue about the relative importance of non-material or ideological agencies, Lenin asserted the decisive primacy of the economic and social structure over legal, political and cultural phenomena. In the final analysis the 'basis' (or 'base') controls the superstructure; the major social transformations of society are consequences of changes in economic structures. Lenin, in describing Marx's thought, says that the 'principal content of Marxism [is] Marx's economic doctrine' (*Karl Marx, SW* 1: 19). This is another cornerstone of Lenin's approach and flows directly from Marx's 'Preface to *A Contribution to the Critique of Political Economy*', where Marx argues that men as producers enter into productive relations entailed in the particular stage in the development of productive forces: these form the base of society to which legal, political and social superstructures correspond (see Lenin, *Karl Marx, SW* 1: 24). Consciousness 'must be explained from the *contradictions of material life*, from the conflict existing between the social forces of production and the relations of production' (Preface to *A Contribution to the Critique of Political Economy*, 1958: 363; italics added).

On this grounding Lenin argues that priority be given to matter over mind and to basis over superstructure. Viewed dialectically, this does not exclude the influence of ideas on matter nor the impact of superstructure on basis; it does, however, put considerable limits on such influence. Lenin saw class struggle as the social dialectic in the laws of historical materialism and he, like Plekhanov, treated seriously the now unfashionable, different 'stages' through which human society develops: these being primitive, communal, slave, feudal, capitalist and communist. The implication here, which must be emphasised, is that socialism is a stage in the development of history, it is an objective necessity, given by the laws of history; socialism is not an 'ideal' social system derived from an ethical subjective evaluation of normative action which underpins non-Marxist Western social-democracy and even much of Western Marxism. Unless this crucial distinction is grasped, the motive forces of Bolshevism cannot be understood.

Lenin attempted to apply this approach to the study of concrete historical conditions. In *The Junius Pamphlet* (1916) Lenin pronounces that 'The Marxist dialectic demands a concrete analysis of each specific historical situation' (*CW* 22: 316). Lenin emphasised the importance of a knowledge of the detail of history and the need to generalise on the basis of empirically verifiable facts, rather than on *a priori* reasoning. *The Development of Capitalism in Russia* is an application of Marx's general analysis of the capitalist mode of production to Russian conditions. Lenin criticises Plekhanov for attempting 'to find answers to specific questions in simple logical developments of general truth. . . . [This] is a vulgarisation of Marxism and a complete mockery of dialectical materialism' (*CW* 3: 32). Lenin here emphasised the importance of taking account of the empirical facts as they emerge in experience. Again, in criticising Trotsky and Bukharin, Lenin makes it clear that one should study concrete conditions rather than bare abstractions. He condemns Bukharin for not conducting a 'concrete study of a particular controversy' (*Once again on the Trade Unions, CW* 32: 94–5). The inner core of the analysis of society is to be found in the contradictory nature of class relationships. As Lukacs (1970) has put it, Lenin 'always related all phenomena to their ultimate basis – *to the concrete actions of . . . [class conditioned] men in accordance with their real class interests*' (1970: 79). The *actual* subjective consciousness of the working class is a conditioned consciousness and is not the same as objective class interest. We shall return later to discuss the problems to which this gives rise.

Marx and Engels used England as their chief empirical referent. Lenin's generalisations were based on his observation of Russian society mainly before the First World War and he related them to the evolution of capitalism as a world social system, as a system whose contradictions would only be resolved by a movement to socialism. By extending Marx's approach and linking it in this way explicitly to Russian problems,* Marxism as it developed in Russia became differentiated from the Marxism of Western Europe.

Lenin emphasised that it is important to examine phenomena from all sides and to see them in the context of the way that they develop: 'in order really to know an object we must study it from all sides [and examine it] in all its connections and "mediations". We shall never achieve this completely, but the demand for all-sidedness is a safeguard against mistakes and rigidity. . . . Dialectical logic demands that we

---

* Trotsky's analysis was much more comparative. See, for example, his discussion of the composition and size of the working class in Germany, England and France (Trotsky 1967: Chapter 1).

consider an object in its development, in its self-movement . . . in its changing state' (*Once again on the Trade Unions, CW* 32: 94). This requires detachment from the situation and an analysis of phenomena from different viewpoints.

He thinks it important to inter-relate general theory and empirical social research. In his discussion of the Austrian journal *Kommunistmus* he rails at purely 'verbal' Marxism: 'G. L.'s article is very Left-wing, and very poor. Its Marxism is purely verbal . . . it gives no concrete analysis of precise and definite historical conditions' (*CW* 31: 165). Lenin stresses that the most essential thing in Marxism, its 'living soul' . . . 'is the concrete analysis of concrete conditions' (*CW* 31: 166). His emphasis is on practical knowledge. In *Materialism and Empirio-Criticism*, Lenin says that 'If we include the criterion of practice in the foundation of the theory of knowledge we inevitably arrive at materialism . . .' (*CW* 14: 140). In his *Philosophical Notebooks*, he makes the well-known point that '*Practice is higher than [theoretical] knowledge*, for it has not only the dignity of universality, but also of immediate actuality' (Conspectus of Hegel's book, *The Science of Logic, CW* 38: 213). In *Statistics and Sociology* Lenin points out that facts have to be considered not in isolation, not as individual 'instances', but in relation to the whole in their interconnectedness (*CW* 23: 272). Lenin's emphasis was on political activity, on practice, based on critical theory and wedded to the empirical study of man in a class-conditioned environment.

This brief description of Lenin's *weltanschauung* should bring out his historical and dialectical materialist approach. But how far is such a viewpoint compatible with the methods and assumptions of the social sciences as they have developed in the West?

LENIN'S METHODOLOGY

As we noted above, Lenin's approach to society developed out of a materialist tradition which was not only held by Marx but was shared by scientists such as Darwin. Hence much in Lenin's methodological approach to society may be traced to a source which is also common to modern Western social science. But it is pertinent to note here that in sociology, as in political science, the revival of interest in Marxism in the 1960s and 1970s excludes a discussion of Lenin as a pioneer of Marxist sociology (Lenin is ignored by Bottomore 1975, Keat and Urry 1975,

Gouldner 1971, Shaw 1975).* Lenin accepted the application of advanced techniques, especially statistics, to collect and analyse empirical data. The *methods* and discoveries of science, like language, are independent of their class uses, and Lenin argued that many of the advances in science should be contained within Marxism. Hence Lenin's Marxism regards the rise of science as being linked to a mode of production and to a class structure, but it is nevertheless a form of liberation from the obscurantism generated by previous modes of production. Western Marxists, in reacting against the use of social and survey data† to legitimate a dominant class, have in my view gone too far in rejecting the methods of science and share much in common with radical liberals, such as Gouldner (1971) and Atkinson (1972), in regarding scientific method as itself being the latest and greatest form of domination.

Lenin's dialectical materialism abandons the explanation of phenomena in terms of cause and effect. As Meyer (1957: 10) has noted, his methodology is a functional approach,‡ in the sense that 'every society is viewed in its totality as a unified organic whole that is larger than all its parts'. Where Lenin differs from non-Marxists and 'bourgeois functionalists' is on the class partiality of social analysis. For Lenin, the application of dialectical materialism to the analysis of society made it the intellectual foundation of socialism in a similar way to that in which the materialism of the natural sciences had been for the evolution of capitalism. It is a general standpoint of Marxism that knowledge is socially conditioned and knowledge which leads away from socialist revolution is an ideological form of false consciousness (Horowitz, in Parekh 1975: 129). Lenin stated quite categorically that there can be no 'impartial' social science in a society where the class struggle continues. 'In one way or another, *all* official and liberal science *defends* wage slavery whereas Marxism has declared relentless war on

---

*At the Annual Conference of the British Sociological Association (1980) celebrating thirty years of British sociology not one paper was concerned with, or discussed, Lenin or Leninism: only one paper mentioned Lenin. Ironically, it is in the field of social policy that some sociologists have seen the relevance of Lenin's views (see Corrigan and Leonard (1978), Navarro (1978) and Ginsburg (1979)). Such writers have been confronted by the practice (rather than the 'theory') of the capitalist state and social-democratic attempts to change it. In the sub-field of the sociology of development some interest has also been shown in Lenin.

† C. Marsh (1980) is one of the very few contemporary Marxists to recognise the importance and relevance of quantitative survey research to sociological analysis.

‡ G. A. Cohen (1978) has trenchantly defended a functionalist interpretation of Marx's thoughts.

that slavery' (*The Three Sources and Three Component Parts of Marxism*, SW 1: 44). Lenin saw social analysis as being connected to class interests and the tasks of Marxists were to identify with, and to promote the cause of, the proletariat. This is a revolutionary practice. *Dialectical* materialism was an ideological force for the proletariat, as materialism had been for the bourgeoisie.

This may be contrasted with a Weberian type of analysis of established institutions and its explanations of change. Weber was not concerned as a social scientist with recommending certain courses of action or political programmes as ethically desirable: science as such does not tell man what he should do, though (of course) sociology can inform man what he rationally should do to achieve certain goals. The Weberian type of analysis takes the form of a 'classification of types of action as tools for the explanation of actual courses of action' (Eldridge: 227). In *Science as a Vocation*, Weber (citing Tolstoy) says that 'Science is meaningless because it gives no answer to the only question important for us "What shall we do and how shall we live?"' ('Science as a Vocation' in Gerth and Mills 1948: 143, cited in Eldridge: 10). Not so for Lenin: he was primarily concerned with answering the question 'What is to be done?' Lenin looked to historical materialism to provide both the goals of, and the means to, action. This involves knowledge of the world and interpretation of it as a *preliminary* to action. In Weber, the notion of 'ethical neutrality' gives a role to social scientists to classify, to explain, to show likely effects of action: goals of action are an individual and personal matter, they are not derived from science, which is agnostic. This was not the position of Lenin, who advocated *ethical activity*, in the sense of social scientists consciously striving to bring about a desired human state which is revealed through the laws of history. This fundamental difference in approach is one of the main reasons why Lenin's thought is alien to Western sociologists and social scientists. Lenin has an inbuilt 'teleological prescience' (see Harding 1977: 37) in his method: given his analysis of developments in society predicated on the Marxist laws of history, he defines the limits of human action and within these he articulates the interests of the proletariat (see, for example, *Three Sources*, SW 1: 45–7).

Lenin was primarily concerned with 'changing the world' rather than interpreting it. As Althusser has cogently put it: in Lenin's political and economic works, 'we can study *Marxist philosophy at work* ... in the "practical" state, Marxist philosophy which has become politics, political action, analysis and decision. Lenin [was] an incomparable *theoreti-*

cal and philosophical formation turned political' (Althusser and Balibar 1970: 76n).

It should by now be clear that this ideological orientation did not mean abandoning a scientific position, as Lenin understood it. He regarded politics as a science: it provided the 'right answers' for political activists who were seeking to overthrow the existing political order and to create a new society. As Lenin put it in a well-known phrase: 'Marxist doctrine is omnipotent because it is true' (*Three Sources, SW* 1: 44). Lenin believed that a Marxist analysis should be informed not only by the demonstrable facts of a situation, but also by their relevance to the general movement of society. The idea of stages of development of the economy is paralleled by social and political developments.

Lenin's view of method in social analysis is quite distinct from a Weberian paradigm of analysis. In the Weberian liberal type of theory, it is presupposed that there are many conflicting interpretations each being more or less true. As Mommsen has put it, 'There did not exist, according to Weber, any "laws" in social reality: at best it was possible to construct law-like conceptualisations of social processes by means of ideal types' (Mommsen 1974: 50) – this is the other side of the coin of scientific agnosticism. Truth is the result of competition between various views in an intellectual free market-place, it involves the free circulation of all ideas and full freedom of criticism. Lenin opposed this. He argued that scientific laws are cumulative. In science, through experiment and practice, some theories are shown to be false and are discarded by the scientific community. Why teach the flat earth theory if it is not true? Propagation of such theories is harmful to science and to mankind. As politics is a science, then it is also true that theories which are shown to be false should also not be intellectual currency, except as part of intellectual history. Lenin makes this view explicit when he criticises opportunism in social democracy. He asserts: 'Those who are really convinced that they have made progress in science would not demand freedom for the new views to continue side by side with the old, but the substitution of new views for the old' (*What is to be Done? SW* 1: 97). Marx put forward a similar viewpoint in *The Critique of the Gotha Program*: 'bourgeois "freedom of conscience" is nothing but the toleration of all kinds of *religious freedom of conscience* . . . and for its part, [the workers' party] endeavours rather to liberate the conscience from the witchery of religion' (Marx, *SW* 2: 33).

The problem here is to know which theories in the social sciences are false. Even if one defines the test of a theory to be in terms of the interests of a class reference group, it is difficult to be sure what are a class's 'real' interests. Lenin's answer was to see the political party of the proletariat articulating this interest. Lenin here anticipates the problem of what Lukes (1974a) has defined as the 'third face of power' (that in which people's interests are obscured or manipulated by the socialisation of values and norms), and he also provides an answer as to how the interest of the proletariat might be articulated.

Lenin sees 'freedom of criticism' to be judged in terms of definite values. Does it promote the development of a 'higher' level of society, does it lead to progress, or does it lead to 'retreat into the marsh' (to use Lenin's own phrase)? For Lenin, progress was defined mainly in class terms: analysis of society had to show how to carry out the destruction of the bourgeoisie and to substitute for it the rule of the proletariat. This in turn leads to a classless society. Just as the natural sciences played an important part in providing an ideological counter to religion in the rise of bourgeois society, so in bourgeois society itself social analysis has an important role in exposing the dominant masking ideology of capitalism.

In this context Lenin advocated rigorous empirical research. To change society one needs to understand it. Lenin did not believe, as do some of his followers and opponents alike, that political or emotional 'commitment' can outweigh an understanding of the facts of a situation, and an explicit policy based on those facts. In *'Left-Wing' Communism – an Infantile Disorder*, he warned against mechanical applications of 'theory' to political events: 'Our theory is not a dogma, but a *guide to action*' (*SW* 3: 336). He argues that 'politics is more like algebra than arithmetic and still more like higher than elementary mathematics' (*ibid.*: 361). While Lenin often disparaged 'bourgeois sociology' he advocated comparative study in a broad sociological sense: 'Science demands, first that the experience of other countries must be taken into account, especially if those other countries, which are capitalist, are undergoing, or have recently undergone, a very similar experience; second, it demands that account be taken of *all* the forces, groups, parties, classes and masses operating in a given country, and also that policy should not be determined only by the desires and views, by the degree of class-consciousness and the militancy of one group or party alone' (*ibid.*: 344).

Nothing could be further from the truth than the assertion that Marxist social analysis is necessarily simplistic, either theoretically or methodologically, because it is a 'class science'. Lenin showed great interest in, and recognised the contribution of, discoveries in physical sciences. Here Lenin follows the tradition of Engels in recognising that 'materialism changes in form with each great scientific discovery' (see discussion in Althusser 1971: 54). He pointed out that one of the shortcomings of materialism before the time of Marx and Engels was the failure to take into account 'the latest developments in chemistry and biology (today it would be necessary to add: and in the electrical theory of matter)' (*Karl Marx, SW* 1: 21).

Lenin paid a great deal of attention to the analysis of 'the facts' – so much so that a New Left Marxist might easily dismiss him as an 'empiricist'. In his discussion of *The Capitalist System of Modern Agriculture* Lenin recognises the major advances that 'social statistics in general and economic statistics in particular' (*CW* 16: 427) had contributed to knowledge. He pointed out that many problems concerning the economic system of modern states and their development could not be analysed 'without taking into account the mass of data about the whole territory of a given country collected according to a single definite programme and summed up by expert statisticians' (*ibid.*). He was one of the first serious students of public voting behaviour: he analysed the election returns to the Second Duma to determine the relative performance of Bolsheviks and Mensheviks against the Socialist Revolutionaries (*The Results of the Elections in the Worker's Curia in Petersburg, CW* 12: 86–7). He devoted considerable attention to the analysis of strike statistics (*Strike Statistics in Russia, CW* 16: 395) and he illustrated the 'objective condition for an immediate mass struggle' by reference to the incidence of strikes (*The Historical Meaning of the Inner-Party Struggle in Russia, CW* 16: 381). (On the use of statistics in Lenin's work see Maslov, 1967.) In his article *Statistics and Sociology* Lenin pointed out the importance of collecting 'precise facts' in order 'to form a proper understanding of a complicated, difficult and often deliberately confused question'. But, and this is the difference from empiricists, he opposed the 'tearing out' of facts from their social context and says that one must search out the theoretical interconnexion between facts (*CW* 23: 272). Such interconnexions could only be given by theory, and hence the underpinning of explanation, couched in terms of historical materialism, distinguishes Marxism–Leninism from positivism. Lenin was not opposed to the use of advanced scientific technique in the social sciences; he pointed out that the movement of technique from the natural to social sciences was not limited to the eighteenth century, but also applied to developments in the nineteenth and twentieth (*CW* 20: 196–7).

The kernel of Lenin's methodology may be summed up as follows. First, he accepted the Marxist laws of dialectical method and historical development: dialectical, in the sense that the objective class contradictions of society both limit man's possible courses of action and provide opportunities for the actor in history; historical, in the sense that history is a progression of modes of production which form parameters to man's action and within which meaningful action must be situated. He regarded Engels as a true interpreter of Marxist analysis; he was not influenced by the writings of the 'young Marx': alienation is a concept which has little place in Lenin's work. He accepted that there was a likelihood that men under capitalism had a false consciousness and he was concerned with *transcending* alienation and false consciousness, not with defining it. Second, he sought to identify in his work with the cause of the proletariat – his work was class conscious in the sense that its goal was to bring about the triumph of the working class through the creation of a socialist society. Third, Lenin inter-related fact and theory. Practice derived from critical theory was applied to objective reality and he linked the subjective perception of reality – the 'action frame of reference' – to the macro analysis of society in terms of universal laws of development. Fourth, Lenin's method of analysis recognised the importance of developments in science of social research and quantitative work, but this had to be situated in the context of Marxist theory.

In the following chapter we turn to consider three major components in Lenin's thought: the notion of uneven development and the role of social classes, the theory of imperialism and the theory of organisation and participation. These three substantive concerns must be seen in relation to each other, and they make up the Bolshevik theory of socialist revolution. On this basis, we shall consider the relevance of Lenin's general approach to the evolution of socialism in Soviet Russia and attempt to relate his theoretical outlook to the context of imperial Russia and the early years of Soviet power. I shall show that there was a unity of thought and practical activity related to the revolutionary situation in Russia. In later chapters of the book, we shall turn to consider how far Lenin's theory and practice was specific to a given society and what role they played in that particular conjuncture of circumstances, that bundle of contradictions, which evolved into Stalinist society.

2

Lenin's theory of revolution

THE POLITICAL IMPLICATIONS OF THE
UNEVEN DEVELOPMENT OF CAPITALISM

Lenin's first and major application of the methods of historical and dialectical materialism is to be found in his study of the development of capitalism in Russia and from this we may illustrate the fact that Lenin's dialectic did not entail a mechanical application of his understanding of the laws of development to a given situation. Rather, he considered empirically the facts of historical development and tried to generalise on the basis of them.

The theory of 'uneven development' is essentially concerned with the rise of advanced forms of capitalist economy and of a proletariat in countries with non-bourgeois *political* formations.* It is an important modification of the idea of stages of modes of production. Marx and Engels were chiefly concerned with, and their model of capitalist development derived from, the economically advanced countries of Western Europe, particularly England and Germany. Lenin, and his comrades in the Russian social-democratic movement, experienced the development of capitalism as it spread from Western Europe to the backward, agrarian, autocratic and mainly Orthodox lands of Tsarist Russia. Lenin's first major work, published in 1899, was a Marxist empirical analysis: *The Development of Capitalism in Russia* (CW3). Here he analysed in terms of Marx's method of the formation of capitalism, the growth of trade in Russia, the development of an internal market, the growth of wage labour and the differentiation of the peasantry.

---

* This is considered here for a society as a whole. Lenin also examined disparate growth internally between regions and sectors of production.

The uneven development of capitalism

The politicial implications of economic growth and social change were always foremost in Lenin's mind. Economic history was not a luxury pursued for its intrinsic academic interest but it was the expression of the different trajectories of societal development followed by various countries. For Lenin, and for the other major Marxist writer on the economic development of Russia, Plekhanov, the growth of capitalism was 'progressive'. This is in keeping with Marx's statement in *The Communist Manifesto* that 'the bourgeoisie, during its rule of scarce one hundred years, has created more massive and more colossal productive forces than have all preceding generations together' (Marx-Engels, SW1: 38). In *The Development of Capitalism in Russia*, Lenin saw in capitalist development not only the 'increase in the productive forces of social labour' (CW3: 595) but also the liberation of labour itself: 'compared with the labour of the dependent or bonded peasant, the labour of the hired worker is a progressive phenomenon in all branches of the economy' (CW3: 598). Russia in the late nineteenth century, argued Lenin, was suffering from two forms of oppression: that to which capitalism gives rise and that derived from relations of personal bondage due to the survival of powerful elements of feudalism. From the latter stemmed the 'abundant survival of ancient institutions that are incompatible with capitalism . . . [and which] immeasurably worsen the condition of the producers, who (to quote Marx) "suffer not only from capitalist production, but also from the incompleteness of its development"' (CW3: 599). The development of capitalism then, under the Tsars, had to be encouraged for it paved the way for the growth of social-democracy and (eventually) for a socialist system of society. Here we already see a policy implication that Russian Marxism had a positive role to play in the development of capitalism which was quite unlike the moral imperative of Marxists in (capitalist) Western Europe. The political conjuncture in Russia was also quite distinct from that of the West.

The rise of social-democracy in Russia took place against the background of the political supremacy of the autocracy and the development of capitalism on the one hand, and against a *Narodnik* or Populist form of socialism on the other. Lenin characterised 'the whole of the history of Russian revolutionary thought during the last quarter of the nineteenth century' as the 'history of the struggle of Marxism against petty-bourgeois Populist socialism' (*Petty-bourgeois and Proletarian Socialism*, CW9: 439). The Populists did not accept that the Marx-Engels scheme of historical materialism could be transposed to Russia. They believed that the individual had considerable possibilities for influencing historical development – one could *prevent* the rise of a capitalist system. They saw social conflict in the wider terms of exploiters and exploited and identified an under-class of toilers (*trudyashchiysya*) rather than a revolutionary class struggle between proletariat and capitalists. Hence they were concerned with the salvation of 'the people' rather than the working class. They argued that a form of socialism could be developed on the basis of the traditional Russian village commune, the *mir*, or *obshchina*. While many conflicting views were held by different advocates of Russian populism, essentially the Populists wanted a classless form of society based on small-scale rural handicraft workshops and near self-sufficient agricultural production; the main production unit would be the landworking peasantry. Most, though by no means all, of the Populists opposed the development of large-scale industrial production and a wage-earning labour force. They felt that the specific conditions of Russia meant that a different 'agrarian' form of socialism could, and should, be developed.

One of the reasons why the Populists were considered by Lenin to be such strong adversaries was to be found in the fact that they considered themselves to be socialists and revolutionaries. All Populists wanted the abolition of the autocracy. Tkachev and Nechaev advocated its overthrow through a clandestine and secret party formed of dedicated revolutionaries. The more right-wing activists, such as Lavrov and Chernov, stressed the educative role of intellectuals and the *khozhdenie v narod* or 'going to the people'. The explanation by intellectuals of exploitation suffered by the people would lead, it was thought, to a spontaneous uprising.

Before considering Lenin's views on class and social stratification, we might anticipate later topics and make some general points concerning common features between Lenin's views and Russian Populism. Firstly, both saw that the intellectuals (and some educated workers) had to bring ideas to the masses. Secondly, the more 'left-wing' group of Populists, like Lenin, stressed the importance of the organisation of the masses for an uprising, and saw dedicated revolutionaries operating through a centrally organised Party. Thirdly, both adopted a flexible view of historical development and recognised the peculiar conditions of Russian socialism. Fourthly, both recognised the importance of the peasants as the key to revolution in Russia. Thus I would argue that Lenin's evolution as a Marxist has to be seen against the *Russian* revolutionary tradition. A strong cultural component is to be found in Lenin's thought which distinguishes Lenin's Marxism from that of

Western European Marxist thought.* It is also important to see this cultural element as infusing other Russian social-democrats. Harding has particularly stressed this point by showing that at certain times there were similarities between Plekhanov, Akselrod and Lenin. (On the hegemony of the proletariat, for instance, see Harding 1977: vol.1, 44–7; 125.) Plekhanov also saw the intelligentsia *in loco parentis* over the workers' movement (see Harding: vol.1, 50–1).

Lenin opposed the methods and objectives of the Populists. He sought to show the extent to which capitalism had penetrated the countryside and the effects it was having on the life of the peasants. The *obshchina* (village community), which his Populist opponents idealised, Lenin considered to be a utopian dream which had no relevance to the Russian countryside of the last quarter of the nineteenth century. Maoists sometimes criticise Lenin on this point, arguing that he failed 'to understand the dynamics of the peasant commune' (Corrigan *et al.* 1978: 56). Whatever may be the virtues of the peasant commune for the Chinese path of socialist development, Lenin saw no positive role for it in Russia at that time. He turned to analyse empirically the class structure of the Russian peasantry. In the preface to the first edition of *The Development of Capitalism in Russia* he saw the 'proletarianisation of the peasantry' being manifest in the formation of a 'huge class of allotment-holding wage-workers' (CW3: 27) and he considered the peasantry to be splitting into two groups: the rich and the poor. By the mid-1890s, Lenin identified three groups: he estimated that half of the peasants were in the 'poor' category having lands inadequate for their needs, while 20 per cent were 'rich' and 30 per cent were middle peasants (CW3: 128). Thus the development of capitalism had gone too far to be checked. Also Lenin endorsed Kautsky's views that capitalism is 'progressive' in agriculture in comparison with pre-capitalist relations and that those who call for the 'consolidation and development of the village community are not socialists at all, but people representing the interests of the big landowners' (Introduction to first edition of *Development of Capitalism in Russia*, CW3: 28).

Lenin then saw a progression to capitalism not only as desirable but as inevitable and given, as it were, by the laws of history, but the course of the trajectory of this development could be influenced by human intervention. While Lenin opposed as utopian any attempt to build socialism

---

* This subject has a long history dating to Martov (1911), it has been developed by Karpovich (1944), Utechin (1960); and Pipes (1960). Many commentators, such as Johnstone (1970), in opposing the political line of these writers have gone too far in rejecting any connexion between Lenin and the Populists.

around the *obshchina,* and he recognised that the development of industrial capitalism was breaking up the feudal social system, he pointed out that the process was quite different from that which had occurred in Western Europe. In Russia, the feudal autocracy was a class which had, to use a contemporary term, 'collaborated' with the Western bourgeoisie. It had encouraged industrial development through the agency of a foreign industrial business class. The major class conflict in Russia was not between a feudal ruling class and a rising capitalist class. The new large-scale industrial development was largely (but not entirely) foreign, and hence capitalism was growing in Russia but without a *Russian* industrial and financial bourgeoisie. Foreign entrepeneurs depended on the autocracy to maintain order through repressive state institutions. Similarly, the autocracy counted on foreign entrepeneurs to provide an industrial infrastructure for Russia to defend herself – to maintain their own class domination. Lenin then located a major locus of socio-political conflict to be between the autocracy and the 'peasantry'. But the Russian peasantry was not a homogeneous grouping and its analysis proved to be one of Lenin's major developments of Marxism.

THE ALLIANCE OF WORKERS AND PEASANTS

Marxists of Western Europe have looked at the peasantry in terms of its role in the bourgeois revolution. In the analysis of the *socialist* revolution, it was regarded as a peripheral group to the class struggle between workers and bourgeoisie. In Russia, however, the leaders of Bolshevik social-democracy saw social change as being closely bound up with the peasants and their problems. What then are the characteristics of the peasants as a social group and how can they be related to Marx's analysis of class?

Marx himself had an ambivalent attitude to the peasantry. In a well-known passage he says that 'each individual peasant family is almost self-sufficient; it itself directly produces the major part of its consumption and thus acquires its means of life more through exchange with nature than in intercourse with society. . . . The great mass of the French nation is formed by simple addition of homologous magnitudes, much as potatoes in a sack of potatoes' (*Eighteenth Brumaire, SW1:* 334).*

* Similarly, Teodor Shanin's 'analytical definition': 'the peasantry consists of small [scale] agricultural producers who, with the help of simple equipment and the labour of their families, produce mainly for their own consumption and for the fulfilment of obligations to the holders of political and economic power' ('The Peasantry as a Political Factor', in Shanin 1971: 240).

The alliance of workers and peasants

For Marx, 'the peasants' formed a class in an economic sense but not in a social and political one. 'In so far as millions of families live under economic conditions of existence that separate their mode of life, their interests and their culture from those of the other classes, and put them in hostile opposition to the latter, they form a class. In so far as there is merely a local interconnexion among these small-holding peasants, and the identity of their interests begets no community, no national bond and no political organisation among them, they do not form a class' (*ibid.*).

Marx in his study of bourgeois revolution in France had been concerned with class conflict and the role of the peasantry. In the February Revolution of 1848, Marx noted that the peasantry joined in establishing the power of Louis Napoleon with the industrial bourgeoisie, industrial proletariat and petty bourgeoisie (*The Class Struggles in France*, SW1: 174). Hence under certain conditions the peasantry would, on the basis of common economic interests, join forces with urban interests against the ruling class. Marx saw, furthermore, that the peasants' economic interests diverged from those of the urban proletariat. The proletariat was a threat to private property and this interest was inimical to the proprietory interest of the peasantry.

On the other hand, in the *Eighteenth Brumaire*, Marx pointed out that the peasant was being savagely exploited by the bourgeoisie and that 'the interests of the peasants are no longer, as under Napoleon, in accord with, but in opposition to, the interests of the bourgeoisie, to capital. Hence the peasants find their natural ally and leader in the *urban proletariat*, whose task is the overthrow of the bourgeois order' (SW1: 338). Here Marx was pointing to the fact that the constant division of land would lead to the deterioration of agriculture; this, together with *capitalist* exploitation of the peasants plus the burden of taxation, would progressively lead them to join forces with the proletariat. Marx, however, did not deal in much detail with the stratification of the peasantry, i.e. the rise of separate strata with distinct economic and political interests.

This point was recognised by Engels. Engels defines four groups in the countryside: the *prosperous peasants*, who belong to the bourgeoisie; the *small peasants*, made up of feudal peasants (still performing *corvée* – unpaid labour-services) and tenant farmers (at the mercy of the landlord); *middle peasants*, 'who farm their own little patches of land' and, though exploited, 'cling tightly to their property' (Prefatory Note to *Peasant War in Germany, SW* 1: 646). Finally, there are the *agricultural labourers*. This group, thought Engels, was becoming 'the most numerous class in the countryside'. As the industrial worker confronts the capitalist, likewise does the agricultural labourer face the landowner. The industrial worker and agricultural labourer have a common class interest in abolishing the private right to property. Engels thought that private property in land could be replaced by 'social property' cultivated by 'co-operative associations of agricultural workers on their common account' (*ibid.*: 647). In Engels's thought, there is a much finer appreciation of the stratification of the peasantry and the possibilities of political action by certain groups in the countryside in alliance with the urban proletariat.

The analysis of Plekhanov and Lenin was predicated on the fact that capitalism was penetrating into the countryside. Rather than viewing 'the peasantry' as a separate economic and social category, as Marx did in the *Eighteenth Brumaire*, they considered the stratification of the peasantry in class terms. Lenin's views on the peasantry then were not something grafted on to Marxist thought, but flowed directly from the economic analysis of Marx and Engels. But Lenin's definition of class could not include the freeholding peasantry as a separate class, or as a group outside other classes. For Lenin, classes were 'large groups of people which differ from each other by the place they occupy in an historically determined system of social production, by their relation (in most cases fixed and formulated in law) to the means of production, by their role in the social organisation of labour, and, consequently, by the dimensions and method of acquiring the share of social wealth of which they dispose. Classes are groups of people, one of which can appropriate the labour of another owing to the different places they occupy in a definite system of social economy' (*A Great Beginning, CW*3: 174).

Lenin rejected the view that the peasantry was a group 'outside' classes – as he defined them. 'The class struggle is the main factor . . . in the sphere of agrarian relations in Russia' (*Agrarian Programme of Russian S-D, CW*6: 148). Essential to Lenin's viewpoint was the dynamic to the stratification of the peasantry. Many he saw as forming a 'stratum of small-scale landowners, of the petty bourgeoisie' (*Petty-bourgeois and Proletarian Socialism, CW* 9: 444). As we noted above, in his study of the development of capitalism in Russia, Lenin had noted that the emancipation of the serfs (in 1861) resulted in the growth of *capitalism* in the countryside, and the struggle of the peasants against what remained of serfdom was also a struggle of the individual peasant for the development of capitalism in agriculture. This process, Lenin believed, was well under way in Russia, and, by virtue of the laws of capitalist economy, would continue. By the same token, however, capitalism in the countryside also led to the pauperisation of many peasants. Such men would either join the ranks of the urban workers or would be compelled to work as wage labour in the countryside and would form a rural proletariat.

The Populist thinkers, on the other hand, looked to the development of the small-scale holdings. In a Marxist sense, they looked 'backwards' to a pre-industrial stage in societal evolution. For Lenin, they were reactionary: identified neither with the proletariat nor with the bourgeoisie (see Meyer: 114–15). In *The Development of Capitalism in Russia*, Lenin made it clear that he thought that with capitalist development this group would decline, that 'the peasantry' would polarise into a group of capitalist farmers and that the vast majority of rural poor would form a rural proletariat. 'Capitalist farming', however, could be achieved in many ways and Lenin was motivated to see that the conditions of capitalism when it arrived would be the most favourable to the political position of the working class. It is in this context that human intervention in the historical process could have positive results.

Hence writers (Corrigan *et al.* 1978: 57) who advocate a form of socialism (in a Marxist sense) based on a development of the *obshchina* (or peasant commune) are completely at variance with Lenin. And I would strongly contest the view often held by such writers that Lenin and the Bolsheviks did not really understand the peasant question in Russia. The peasantry formed a major part of the study of Russia in the work of Lenin (and here he followed in the footsteps of Plekhanov's *Our Differences*). Though it is true that some of Lenin's predictions about the class differentiation of the peasantry *after* 1917 turned out to be false, we cannot overlook the fact that Lenin was the first major Marxist to give the peasantry an important place in a theory of revolution.

Lenin characterised four groups in the countryside: the landed gentry, the petty bourgeoisie (peasants with a small plot, selling on the market), the poor mainly subsistence peasants, and the rural proletariat. This is similar to Engels's classification. It was clear that the landed gentry was a prop to the existing regime and that the rural proletariat could be considered to be part of the working class. But how would the dynamics of capitalist development affect these groups? One possibility would be the development of agriculture on the 'junker' pattern: the hereditary gentry turning into a capitalist landowning class by developing agricultural production through wage labour, capital utilisation and production for the market. This would give rise to a state, possibly with a military form, which would be controlled by the new junker landlord class. The alternative was the 'American' pattern: the gentry would be destroyed and a class of agricultural freeholders would spring from the peasant petty-bourgeoisie. The greater equality of the rural population would be more conducive to a popular government and a bourgeois-democratic type of government. Lenin favoured this latter form of development: it would completely eradicate the vestiges of feudalism and it would prevent the rise of a Bonapartist state – which would use its force against liberal-democracy, and particularly the emergent workers' movement.

The unfolding process of history meant that the next stage in Russian history, in a Marxist sense, would be the bourgeois revolution. This would help rid Russia of feudal fetters arresting the rise of capitalism. 'In order to clear the road for the free development of class warfare in the village, it is necessary to remove all remnants of the feudal order which are at present *covering up* the beginnings of capitalist antagonism within the rural population and are preventing them from developing' (*The Agrarian Programme, CW6*: 148). Marx and Engels had considered the peasantry *ex post facto* in their role in the bourgeois revolution in France. In Lenin's theory, the peasantry (or rather various strata of it) was to play a crucial role in both bourgeois and socialist revolutions.

THE BOURGEOIS REVOLUTION

How then would the bourgeois revolution occur? In considering this question Lenin made some interesting adaptations of Marxism to the analysis of the development of capitalism. In Russia, he argued, one could not expect the capitalist class unaided to overthrow the autocracy. Lenin criticised the Menshevik view of the proletariat standing aside and letting the contradiction of capitalism develop as a mechanical application of Marxism. The dialectical and historical approach of Lenin was a much more flexible tool of analysis than that adopted by his opponents. The unique development of historical forces, the overlapping of modes of production called for a new synthesis of the development of the productive forces in Russia.

The Mensheviks adopted the following and traditional line of reasoning universally accepted by Marxists in the West at that time. Socialism could only be created out of an advanced capitalist society. The laws of historical materialism taught that the development of material forces came into conflict with relations of production (i.e. class relations) only at an advanced stage of the mode of production. Before capitalism was 'ripe' for socialism, it would be premature for the working class to attempt to seize power. Such an attempt might fail but, even if it did succeed, it would not result in socialism. (This is the argument utilised by Marxist opponents of Bolshevism down to the present day.) Russia was a feudal power undergoing early capitalist development. The capitalist class was the ascendant class in Russia and the destiny of this class was to abolish feudalism. The proletariat could help bring about the bourgeois revolution – it could assist the bourgeoisie by disrupting Tsarism, but could not lead a bourgeois revolution. Social democracy had to play a waiting game. It would take a leading role on the stage of history only after the bourgeois revolution. In a democratic republic, where trade unions would develop, the Party would have a mass character and then the working class would engage in a revolutionary struggle against capital. Clearly, the Mensheviks had in mind the ideal model of the large social-democratic parties and unions of Western Europe, who were fighting the bourgeoisie on its own terms. Theirs was the more orthodox Marxist outlook, at least in terms of Western European Marxism.

Lenin, following other Russian Marxists such as Akselrod, Plekhanov and Trotsky, did not share this view and his own theories led to a significant shift in Marxist theory as applied to developing countries in the twentieth century. Under the conditions of Tsarist Russia, the industrial bourgeoisie was politically impotent; it was unlikely to lead a bourgeois revolution. This was the result of the peculiar development of capitalism in Russia which resulted in the evolution of two leading groups of industrial capitalists: those abroad and those in Russia. Neither was likely to play a leading or hegemonic role in the capitalist revolution.

The (Western) magnates of capitalism, to be sure, would have preferred a liberal-democratic society like the ones in which they flourished at home and the abolition of the autocracy as a system of rule. But the foreign bourgeoisie was also under the political 'protection' of the autocracy, which gave to foreign capital financial privileges and often a guaranteed rate of return on capital. The foreign bourgeoisie did not participate directly in the internal Russian political arena. As long as its capital was preserved and enlarged it would lack any revolutionary dynamic and it could not be considered a revolutionary force able to overthrow the autocracy.

The Russian bourgeoisie, for its part, was weak both in numbers and in confidence. Unlike the capitalist West, Russia lacked a strong trading, commercial and manufacturing class, though she had a vocal liberal intelligentsia. Liberal Russian writers such as Pestel, Tolstoy and Herzen emphasised values of individual freedom and the liberation of the peasant. Their ideology was democratic rather than bourgeois. They deplored the development of industrial capitalism and advocated the retention of traditional socialistic elements in Russian life, particularly the peasant commune. Russia's indigenous business class, while growing in numbers and importance in the late nineteenth and early twentieth centuries, was nowhere comparable to its counterpart in Western Europe, and while Russia had many creative writers advocating democratic ideals, the business class had not produced a theorist such as Adam Smith, Ricardo or Marshall to rationalise and legitimate their activity.

The small urban Russian bourgeoisie not only lacked intellectual leadership but also was confronted by the rising urban working class. It was shielded from factory unrest by the Tsarist authorities; while the conditions may have been irksome, there was nevertheless security of property. Participation in revolution may have led to an upheaval the results of which would have been more threatening – the bourgeoisie would have been faced with an implacable foe in the working class. Lenin could not see this group leading a capitalist revolution and he concluded that under its own steam the industrial and commercial bourgeoisie would neither lead nor complete the bourgeois revolution.

In analysing the forces of bourgeois revolution under the autocracy, Lenin's analysis hinged on the petty-bourgeois peasantry. He saw evolving from the peasant masses a stratum of smallholders – a yeoman farmer class – and he came to realise that the peasants' demand for land had a bourgeois revolutionary potential. In the light of this, the strategy of the social-democrats in the bourgeois-democratic revolution appeared paradoxical. The urban workers would provide the political leadership to the bourgeois-democratic revolution. Lenin emphasised the potentiality of the metal-workers employed in large-scale factory production. These were the workers with deeper roots in the working class, with higher levels of skill and education, their greater mass and density gave rise through direct communication to higher levels of political consciousness. Lenin in *The Development of Capitalism in Russia* regarded the proletariat in the heavy machine industry as being subject to the most advanced forms of capitalist economy (*CW*3: 584).

Thus social-democracy should 'concentrate its activities on the industrial proletariat, who are most susceptible to social-democratic ideas, most developed intellectually and politically, and most important by virtue of their number and concentration in the country's large political centres' (*The Tasks of the Russian Social-Democrats*, *CW*2: 330). The development of industrial labour in the factory brought head-on the conflict between capital and labour (which was muted in the countryside) and the factory provided lines of communication between workers. This made the working class the vanguard which could express all the grievances of the oppressed in Russia. It was for the social-democratic party to provide *leadership*, to articulate a working-class interest. Lenin contrasts the Narodnik view that Russia's 'man of the future' is the *muzhik*, to that of the social-democrats who saw in the (factory) worker the 'man of the future': the worker 'is none other than the foremost representative of the entire exploited population' (*What the 'Friends of the People' Are*, *CW*1: 299). Lenin saw leadership as being about the creation of new possibilities given by circumstances. He criticised his opponents for having a retrospective theory – of analysing why things had happened as they did – rather than theory exploiting new future possibilities.

In the bourgeois revolution the working class and peasantry shared the same short-term political goals. The task of Russian social-democracy was 'to help the peasants in the most energetic fashion, help them finally and completely to throw off the rule of the officials and the landlords' (*Petty-bourgeois and Proletarian Socialism*, *CW*9: 442). This was a struggle of the peasantry against the traditional landowners and the remnants of serfdom. From the point of view of immediate political strategy, the bourgeois-democratic and revolutionary forces of the peasantry had to be supported – and this included the expropriation of the landlord's estates. 'The proletariat must carry the democratic revolution to completion, allying to itself the mass of the peasantry in order to crush the autocracy's resistance by force and paralyse the bourgeoisie's instability. The proletariat must accomplish the socialist revolution, allying to itself the mass of semi-proletarian elements of the population, so as to crush the bourgeoisie's resistance by force and paralyse the instability of the peasantry and the petty-bourgeoisie' (*Two Tactics SW*1: 494).

It must be emphasised that this was not a socialist revolution: the working class (or rather its political arm, the social-democratic party) had to lead the bourgeois revolution. 'A bourgeois revolution is *absolutely* necessary to the interests of the proletariat' (*SW1*: 452). Lenin turned by analogy to the Paris Commune of 1871: its leaders were unable to 'distinguish between the elements of a democratic revolution and a socialist revolution . . . [it was] a government that confused the tasks of fighting for a republic with those of fighting for socialism. . . . It was a Government *such as ours should not be*' (*Two Tactics*, *SW1*, 478).

The social-democrats had also to participate in the revolutionary government to secure for the Russian people (including the working class) the rights which the bourgeoisie promised. The results of the 1848 Revolution in France had shown that bourgeois rule need not be of the liberal-democratic kind, but could lead to capitalism within the framework of dictatorship and authoritarianism – as the rule of Louis Napoleon had brought home. This policy again illustrates the way that the intelligentsia had to play an active role in leading the revolutionary movement by learning from history.

The alliance with the petty bourgeoisie would be a temporary one, until the autocracy had been abolished and the bourgeoisie firmly established as a dominant class within a democratic republic. 'The workers wage the democratic struggle together with a section of the bourgeoisie – especially the petty-bourgeoisie. . . . The struggle against the officials and the landlords can and must be waged together with all the peasants, even the well-to-do and middle peasants. On the other hand, [the struggle for socialism is waged] against the bourgeoisie and therefore against the well-to-do peasants, [it] can only be waged in a reliable manner together with the rural proletariat' (*Petty-bourgeois and Proletarian Socialism*, CW9: 443). In the bourgeois revolution there would be a temporary alliance for, after the overthrow of Tsarism, the interests of rich (and possibly middle) peasants and proletariat diverged. The proletariat opposed the property interests of the peasantry. 'In its struggle against the bourgeoisie, the class of small producers, including the small farmers is a *reactionary* class, and therefore trying to save the peasantry by protecting small-scale farming and small-holdings from the onslaught of capitalism would be a useless retarding of social development; it would mean deceiving the peasantry with illusions of the possibility of prosperity even under capitalism; it would mean disuniting the labouring classes and creating a privileged position for the minority at the expense of the majority' (*Agrarian Programme*, CW6:114).

Here then we may summarise Lenin's contentions. In a country confronted with early (imperialist) capitalist development, where the industrial and commerical bourgeoisie was weak, the proletariat (through the Party) had the mission to lead the bourgeois revolution. 'The activity of the working class will set the bourgeoisie in motion to make the bourgeois revolution.' To understand fully Lenin's appraisal of social change (of pushing forward the wheels of history) we must also consider his analysis of class alliances and his views on Party organisation.

Before turning to these latter two subjects we may sketch in some of the actual events of 1905, and consider how Lenin's thinking changed between 1905 and 1917. In 1905 the first major revolutionary upheaval occurred. Numerous revolts broke out in Russia: in towns, Soviets were formed and there were mass strikes; in the villages there were numerous instances of political violence directed against state officials and landowners. Mensheviks harried the established powers, supported strikes, encouraged, but did not lead, revolutionary upheavals. The Bolsheviks led popular uprisings, such as those in Moscow – but were not able to hold on to power (for details, see Lane 1975: Chapter 4). The Tsar gave concessions and in the October Manifesto promised a liberal-democratic constitution. At this stage the urban bourgeoisie turned and joined with the autocracy against the insurgents. The army remained loyal, and the insurgents were defeated. Though the power of the Tsar was weakened, a bourgeois-democratic revolution did not take place.

PERMANENT REVOLUTION

In the wake of the 1905 Revolution, an even more radical adaptation of Marxist theory was being put by two non-Bolsheviks: Trotsky and Parvus. Their argument took into account similar trends in Russian history to those recognised by Lenin. Not only did they agree that the Russian bourgeoisie was incapable of revolutionary leadership of the bourgeois revolution, but they advocated that the working class should lead and *carry through* the bourgeois revolution to the socialist stage. This was the idea of *permanent revolution*, which envisaged that the bourgeois revolution would be impossible to contain, once it had been started by the working class, and would pass over to the socialist stage. 'Once having won power, the proletariat cannot keep within the limits of bourgeois democracy. It must adopt the tactics of *permanent revolution*, i.e. must destroy the barriers between the minimum and the maximum programme of Social-Democracy, go over to more and more radical social reforms and seek direct and immediate support in revolution in Western Europe' (Trotsky, *Results and Prospects*, 1962: 163). Trotsky and Parvus emphasised that the development of capitalism in Russia led to the most advanced industrial enterprises being built in a most backward country. Russia then had the most highly exploited and most class conscious proletariat in Europe. 'In a country economically backward, the proletariat can take power earlier than in countries where capitalism is advanced. . . . The Russian Revolution produces conditions, in which power may . . . pass into the hands of the proletariat *before* the politicians of bourgeois liberalism have had the chance to show their statesman-like genius to the full' (Trotsky 1962: 195).

The liberals, in Trotsky's view, were unable to lead a resurrection and would compromise with the autocracy (for a detailed discussion, see Knei-Paz 1978: 34–41). Trotsky always considered the peasantry to be a politically primitive or bourgeois force – it could not be relied on by the proletariat in its struggle for socialism. While the agrarian problem remained a source of revolutionary agitation on the part of the peasants, he believed that they were incapable of organised rebellion – their 'cretinous localism' could lead only to peasant risings, not to revolution (see discussion in Knei-Paz 1978: 41–7). The peasantry would have to rely on, and would look to, the working class to lead the revolution.

The working class by virtue of its rapid growth, concentration and relative homogeneity was highly class conscious. It could head not only the bourgeois but also the socialist revolution.

With the proletariat taking the lead in the overthrow of the feudal power, the revolution would pass through the capitalist stage. There would be a telescoping of stages and a proletarian dictatorship would be established. 'The dictatorship of the proletariat appears not *after* the completion of the democratic revolution . . . for in that case it would simply be impossible in Russia. . . . The dictatorship of the proletariat appeared probable and even inevitable on the basis of the bourgeois revolution, precisely because there was no other power and no other way to solve the tasks of the agrarian revolution. But exactly this opens up the prospect of a democratic revolution growing over into the socialist revolution' (*Permanent Revolution*, 1962: 58). There would be a dictatorship of the proletariat *before* it was a majority; and this would be achieved without an alliance with the peasantry.

Trotsky distinguished between a national revolution, in which the autocracy would be overthrown as a result of all revolutionary forces, and a class revolution which would be dominated by the working class. An alliance between proletariat and peasantry could not last because the obligations of the urban working class to the agricultural proletariat would be actively opposed by the bourgeois peasantry. In the towns the introduction of the eight-hour day and measures for alleviating unemployment would lead to a clash with the urban bourgeoisie. The national coalition which achieved the overthrow of the autocracy would disintegrate in the face of the policies which the working class would institute. Trotsky then argued that a process of 'uninterrupted revolution' would occur. The national uprising would lead to socialist revolution (see Knei-Paz 1978:127–40).

As we have seen above, Lenin in 1905 disagreed with this 'merging' of bourgeois and socialist revolutions: he saw the two as distinct, with the socialist following the bourgeois and having a different constellation of class forces. But Lenin saw these stages running into each other. In September 1905 Lenin said that 'We stand for un-interrupted revo-lution' (*S-D's Attitude toward the Peasant Movement*), which Brym (1978:102) interprets to mean: 'for the immediate extension of the revolution to its second socialist stage'. At this time, however, this is to misinterpret Lenin. Lenin made it clear in this pamphlet that social-democracy could proceed 'from the democratic revolution', only 'in accordance with the measure of our strength, the strength of the class-conscious and organised proletariat' (*ibid.*). The revolution would be uninterrupted in the sense that after a bourgeois-democratic revo-lution, a struggle for socialism would continue uninterrupted. Trotsky went much further than Lenin: the formal capitalist stage could be avoided. The proletariat could, as it were, leap-frog over it. Between 1905 and 1917 Lenin's tactical approach and analysis of the dynamics of socialist revolution were to move more towards Trotsky's position. The 1905 upheavals had shown the impotence of the bourgeoisie, which did not push the revolution to its conclusion, and Lenin began to realise that, even with the leadership of the proletariat, the bourgeoisie was unwilling and unable to overthrow the autocracy. During the 1905

Revolution, like Trotsky, Lenin did not believe that the peasants could act as an independent revolutionary force.

Before the First World War, Lenin did not consider the time to be ripe for going over to the socialist stage. This would only come *after* the bourgeois revolution was completed. The important objective was to further the alliance of the proletariat and the peasantry and he criticised Trotsky for neglecting the crucial role of the peasantry. Trotsky, he said, took over from the Bolsheviks 'their call for a decisive proletarian revolutionary struggle and for the conquest of political power by the proletariat, while from the Mensheviks it has borrowed "repudiation" of the peasantry's role' (*On the Two Lines in the Revolution*, CW21: 419–20). The task of the Party was to draw the peasants into revolutionary activity, with their aid Tsarism would be overcome, then the proletariat would use its freedom 'not to aid the prosperous peasants in their struggle against the village workers but for the completion of a socialist revolution with the proletarians of Europe' (*ibid.*). This quotation illustrates that Lenin now began to think that the bourgeois revolution could grow into the socialist, and that Lenin's ideas in practice were moving towards the idea of permanent revolution. Lenin, however, even in 1905, emphasised the reciprocal effects of revolution in Russia and Europe: 'We shall succeed in ensuring that the Russian revolution is not a movement of a few months, but a movement of many years; that it leads, not merely to a few paltry concessions from the powers that be, but to the complete over-throw of those powers. . . . And if we succeed in achieving this, then . . . the revolutionary conflagration will spread to Europe: the European worker languishing under bourgeois reaction, will rise in his turn and show us "how it is done", then the revolutionary upsurge in Europe will have a repercussive effect upon Russia and will convert an epoch in a few revolutionary years into an era of several revolutionary decades' (*S-D and the Provisional Revolutionary Government*, CW8: 287–8). Both Trotsky and Lenin, even during the 1905 Revolution, saw that a revolution in Russia was an international phenomenon.

Unlike Trotsky, Lenin gave an important role to the peasantry, which he saw as part of the revolutionary masses. Here, of course, there are similarities with the Populists. After the 1905 Revolution, Lenin began to conceive of the proletariat and petty-bourgeois peasantry bringing about a 'revolutionary-democratic dictatorship of the proletariat and peasantry', which would 'kindle the socialist revolution in Europe'. If the petty bourgeoisie supported the proletariat then it could 'assume the leadership of the bourgeois Russian revolution' (*Several theses,*

CW21: 402–3). Lenin recognised that the peasantry's demand for the seizure and division of land was not socialist: it was 'reactionary and utopian from the view-point of socialism' but it was 'revolutionary from the point of view of bourgeois democratisation' (*The Fifth Congress of the RSDLP*, CW12: 466). The peasant revolution would destroy what remained of feudalism: 'The more complete the victory of the peasantry, the sooner will the proletariat stand out as a distinct class, and the more clearly will it put forward its purely socialist tasks and aims' (*ibid.*). In the socialist revolution the ally of the Russian proletariat (rural as well as urban) would be the international working class. 'For the task [of carrying out the democratic revolution in Russia] our ally is the petty-bourgeois peasantry of Russia; for the task [of kindling the socialist revolution in Europe] it is the proletariat of other countries' (*Several theses*, CW21). As early as 1907, then, Lenin's class alliances were set. By 1917 the world had changed and Lenin had added another formal dimension to his theoretical armoury: imperialism.

IMPERIALISM

The analysis we have pursued so far has linked Lenin's theories to the evolution of Tsarist Russia. The 'uneven development' of capitalism has two sides: not only that of the rise of capitalism in an undeveloped country, but also the dynamics of capitalism on a world scale. Whereas Lenin's analysis of capitalism had Russia at the centre of his frame of reference, for Trotsky the world order of capitalism was always at the fore of his concern. Trotsky, even in 1905/6, recognised the advantage of backwardness for the immediate political victory of the proletariat in Russia, but he quite logically saw that this alone could not guarantee the victory of socialism. In *Results and Prospects* (1906) he declared: 'Without the direct state support of the European proletariat, the working class of Russia cannot remain in power and convert its temporary dominance into a lasting socialist dictatorship.' The idea that imperialism would snap at its 'weakest link' ante-dated Lenin's views, expounded in his treatise on *Imperialism, the Highest Form of Capitalism* (written 1916). As Knei-Paz points out, Parvus had put forward this view as early as 1904: 'The world process of capitalist development brings about a political upheaval in Russia. In turn, this will affect political developments in all capitalist countries. The Russian revolution will shake the capitalist world. And the Russian proletariat will assume the role of the vanguard of the social revolution' (Parvus, *Rossiya i revolyutsiya*, 1906: 133, cited by Knei-Paz 1978: 18; see discussion *ibid.*: 16–9; 160–1). Trotsky's inventiveness as a Marxist theorist consisted in linking this idea to that of the proletariat seizing power *first* in the underdeveloped country, with a feedback effect then bringing down the advanced capitalist states; consequently, workers' governments would help eradicate the many forms of backwardness on a world scale. Here then Trotsky mapped out during the 1905 Revolution a strategy for socialist revolution which has become a dominant political force in the twentieth century. He foresaw the shift of the fulcrum of revolutionary forces from the West to the East. But he also emphasised the fact that the triumph of socialism could not be achieved independently of a revolution in the advanced capitalist states.

Lenin's own views on imperialism developed in a more piecemeal fashion. In *The Development of Capitalism in Russia* Lenin investigated empirically the effects of world capitalism on Russia. His analysis led to the conclusion that the bourgeois revolution was imminent in Russia. Lenin's focus was always on Russia, whereas Trotsky's vision was of capitalism as a world system. Lenin's analysis in *Imperialism* grew out of the experience of the First World War. He came to consider that the contradictions of capitalism had led the Western European states to the verge of collapse. This signalled not only the defeat of the Tsarist order but also justified the Russian proletariat in taking the first step in the direction of building socialism. Now the conditions in Western Europe had changed and Lenin in effect was adopting Trotsky's earlier analysis. Unlike Trotsky, however, Lenin did advance a formal theory of imperialism.

The term 'imperialism' was used to describe British capitalism before Lenin adopted it to characterise world capitalism. J. A. Hobson's *Imperialism*, written in 1902, was a liberal critique of British foreign trade policy. Its level and method of analysis and the conclusions it made are quite different from Lenin's and it is most confusing and inaccurate to bracket together a 'Hobson–Lenin theory' of imperialism. Hobson saw the stimulus for the search for foreign markets to be derived from motives of 'pride, pugnacity and prestige'. Some vested interests then, according to Hobson, were in support of British ideas of national grandeur and these saw Empire and the foreign trade that went with it as a source of strength. The spread of capitalism is associated with the founding of colonies which are politically dependent on European states. Hobson opposed these politically imperialist groups on the grounds that it was a weakness to be overcommitted to foreign trade: only a minority gained from it and Hobson argued that it prevented consumption from rising at home. The home market, he felt, could provide for indefinite expansion. Hobson then, in opposing 'imperialism', was antithetical not to the capitalist system as such, but to strata of it whom he thought benefited from the imperial connexion. There is thus no Marxist class conflict in Hobson, but a liberal-democratic analysis of opposing 'interests'.

For Lenin, 'imperialism' had a much wider economic and political connotation. Russia was not a political colony, but it was part of the system of capitalist imperialism. The term 'imperialism' referred to the developments which were taking place in the world system of capitalism: these developments were concerned both with the internal dynamics of the advanced capitalist societies and with the relations between the advanced and backward countries.

Marx and Engels had not explicitly formulated a theory of imperialism, though they did point to the world-wide spread of capitalism. In the *Communist Manifesto* they wrote:

The bourgeoisie has through its exploitation of the world market given a cosmopolitan character to production and consumption in every country. . . . The bourgeoisie, by the rapid improvement of all instruments of production, by the immensely facilitated means of communication, draws all, even the most barbarian, nations into civilization. . . . It compels all nations, on pain of extinction, to adopt the bourgeois mode of production; it compels them to introduce what it calls civilization into their midst, i.e. to become bourgeois themselves. In one word, it creates a world after its own image. (Marx-Engels, *SW*1: 38)

In his discussion of British rule in India, Marx again made clear his view that British rule would bring about a 'social revolution' in India, and he pointed to the traditional subjugation of the local population under the 'solid foundation of Oriental despotism' (*Future Results of British-Rule in India, SW*1: 351, 350). In Marx's opinion British capital investment in the railway network would result in the economic development of India. 'You cannot maintain a net of railways over an immense country without introducing all those industrial processes necessary to meet the immediate and current wants of railway locomotion, and out of which there must grow the application of machinery to those branches of industry not immediately connected with railways. The railway system will therefore become, in India, truly the forerunner of modern industry.' (*British Rule in India*, SW1: 355–6). Marx went on to conclude that 'Bourgeois industry and commerce create these material conditions of a new world in the same way as geological revolutions have created the surface of the earth' (*ibid.*: 358).

This tendency of capitalism to expand from a European base to a world-wide phenomenon involving the founding of colonies has been seen by many Marxists and non-Marxists alike to be one of the most significant developments of the late nineteenth century. For Marxists, however, colonialism is only one aspect, or a special case, of imperialism. Lenin was more directly influenced by Hilferding (*Finance Capital*, 1910) and Bukharin (*The World Economy of Imperialism*, 1914). For Lenin, imperialism is an advanced stage of capitalism; not only does it have its roots in the economic development of the European capitalist societies, but it has wide implications for the class struggle and revolution in the contemporary world. He defines it as 'capitalism in that stage of development in which domination of monopoly and finance capital has taken shape; in which the export of capital has acquired pronounced importance; in which the division of the world by international trusts has begun; and in which the partition of all territory of the earth by the greatest capitalist countries has been completed' (*Imperialism*, CW22: Chapter 7). This definition contains five major points: the growing concentration of production and capital with oligopoly taking the place of free competition; the merging of bank and industrial capital with the growing domination of bank capital; the export of capital replacing the export of commodities; the division of the world among international capitalist combines; and the completion of the territorial division of the world between capitalist powers.

As Kemp (1967) and others have pointed out, Lenin's theory of imperialism is thoroughly grounded in a Marxist analysis of society and cannot be understood independently of it. It is generally recognised by Marxists that there are three major tendencies in capitalist society which give rise to imperialism. First, as a 'closed system' the process of capitalist development entails the extraction of surplus value (or profit) which creates an insufficiency of demand, leading to slumps in industrial production. Second, technical change increases the proportion of constant to variable capital; the organic composition of capital rises. This results in a falling rate of profit. Third, competition leads to the decline of independent small firms with individual entrepeneurs and to the rise of joint stock companies with paid managers. With these structural changes come parallel developments in finance: the banks become dominant sources of capital and finance.

These three tendencies in the advanced countries provide the underlying dynamic to the theory of imperialism worked out by Lenin in *Imperialism*. A major emphasis in Lenin's work is that the contradictions of capitalism become international in character. Imperialism helps to explain why the revolution of the working class is postponed in the advanced countries, why the tendency of the rate of profit to fall is reversed, and why the centre of the revolutionary arena has moved to the developing countries. The rich European nations expand at the expense of the poor countries who provide them with cheap materials, markets for commodities and excess capital, and a source of cheap labour. The export of capital in turn speeds up the development of capitalism in the underdeveloped countries, and the collapse of the capitalist system is staved off. The state and the banking system co-ordinate the capital market.

Lenin was not concerned with the economic changes of the capitalist system *per se* but with their effects and their implications for revolutionary activity. As Lukacs has pointed out, Lenin's superiority as a Marxist thinker lies in his ability to connect the economic theory of imperialism to 'every political problem of the present epoch, thereby making the economics of the new phase a guide-line for all concrete action in the resultant decisive conjuncture' (Lukacs 1970: 41). What then are the effects of these economic tendencies on the revolutionary struggle?

There are three major sets of implications. First, the economic benefits of imperialism ensure the loyalty of the masses, including the working class, to the capitalist state in the rich imperialist states. Lenin quotes Cecil Rhodes who, after hearing speeches by unemployed London workers, wrote: 'we colonial statesmen must acquire new lands to settle the surplus population, to provide new markets for the goods produced in the factories and mines. The Empire, as I have always said, is a bread and butter question. If you want to avoid civil war, you must become imperialists' (Rhodes cited by Lenin, *Imperialism*, CW22: 257). The super-profits obtained from the labour of those in the underdeveloped world provides the economic prop to the 'affluent workers' of the imperialist states. Such groups of the proletariat indirectly exploit the labour of the toilers in the underdeveloped lands. 'Out of such enormous super-profits (since they are obtained over and above the profits which capitalists squeeze out of the workers of their "own" country) it is *possible to bribe* the labour leaders and the upper stratum of the labour aristocracy. . . . The capitalists of the "advanced countries" . . . are bribing [the workers] in a thousand different ways, direct and indirect, overt and covert' (*Imperialism*, CW22: 193–4). Workers' political parties and trade unions want to obtain the maximum share in imperialist profits and therefore support the ruling classes of their nation. Lenin, then, provides an explanation of Engels's thesis of the bourgeoisification of the English working class. 'The English proletariat is becoming more and more bourgeois, so that this most bourgeois of all nations is apparently aiming ultimately at the possession of a bourgeois aristocracy and a bourgeois proletariat as well as a *bourgeoisie*. For a nation which exploits the whole world this is, of course, to a certain extent justifiable' (Engels to Marx, Oct. 1858, cited in *Imperialism*, CW22: 283).

The second political development stemming from Lenin's analysis of imperialism has to do with the corruption of working-class consciousness by the struggles *between* the imperialist countries. Workers' political parties (and unions) in the advanced countries seize on the short-term maximisation of their economic interests by supporting their governments' foreign claims. Competition between national capitals for colonies and areas of influence and for the annexation of available lands leads to war. 'The war of 1914–18 was on both sides an imperialist (annexationalist, predatory and plunderous) war for the partition of the world and for the distribution and redistribution of colonies, of spheres of influence of finance, capital etc.' (*Imperialism*, CW22: 189–90).* Lenin believed that world war led to the crisis of capitalism and the workers in the advanced states would begin to perceive the real nature of class relationships. Indeed, it was the observation of the world war which had given the impetus for Lenin to study imperialism. The 1914 World War had the effect, not only of concentrating the effects of imperialism in a dramatic and violent conflict, but it would also, thought Lenin, transform the subjective consciousness of the Western European working class. 'The imperialist war is ushering in the era of social revolution. All the objective conditions of recent times have put the proletariat's revolutionary mass struggle on

* This quotation is from the Preface to the French and German editions, written in July, 1920.

the order of the day' (*Draft Resolution at Zimmerwald, CW*21: 347). Lenin was not pessimistic about the chances of revolution in Western Europe. Imperialism could at best postpone the crash of European capitalism, it could not prevent it.

The third implication for political action in the twentieth century is that Lenin's *Imperialism* located the class struggle in an international perspective. The collapse of the world system of capitalism might *first* occur in the backward countries, and the imperialist chain might snap at its weakest link. Exploitation of the working class is on a world scale and the class struggle transcends national boundaries. The export of capital speeds up the development of capitalism in the receiving countries and is conducive to the rise of a class-conscious working class: Russia was a paradigmatic case. In such countries the possibilities of bribing the workers are fewer. In addition the indigenous bourgeoisie is weaker. Lenin's theory of imperialism thus entails, and this was made explicit after 1917, that the proletarians of the backward nations become the bearers of 'consciousness', as it were, of the working class. Once the workers and poor peasants of these countries rebelled, there would be a 'feedback' on the workers in the West, who themselves would follow. This then was Lenin's justification for the seizure of power by a socialist party in a society having recently entered the capitalist stage of production. In such a country as Russia, the proletariat – led by the Bolshevik Party – could seize power and this would spark off a world revolution and the collapse of capitalism in the more advanced countries.

In February 1917, the Russian autocracy collapsed. The proletariat and bourgeoisie did not seize power – the autocracy relinquished power. For Lenin this indicated the end of the feudal political structure, and now he argued that the time had come to go forward to begin the *socialist* revolution because 'The bourgeois revolution in Russia is completed'. 'According to the old conception, the rule of the proletariat and peasantry, their dictatorship, can and must *follow* the rule of the bourgeoisie. In real life, however things have turned out otherwise; an extremely original, new, unprecedented *interlocking of one and the other* has taken place. Side by side, together and simultaneously, we have *both* the rule of the bourgeoisie . . . and the revolutionary-democratic dictatorship of the proletariat and the peasantry, which *voluntarily* cedes power to the bourgeoisie and voluntarily makes itself an appendage of the bourgeoisie' (*Letters on Tactics, CW*24: 45–6). The proletariat must go on the offensive: 'The only solution is for power to be in the hands of the proletariat, and for the latter to be supported by the poor peasants or semi-proletarians' (*On Slogans*, CW25: 189). In Lenin's view, the revolution in Russia would be a spark which would lead to the proletarian revolution in the West; it was the beginning of the world proletarian revolution. In April 1917, he declared on arrival from Europe: 'The robbers' imperialistic war is the beginning of civil war in Europe. . . . Any day may come the crash of European imperialism. The Russian Revolution [i.e. the February Revolution], which you have carried out, has laid the foundation for it and opened a new epoch. Long live the world-wide socialist revolution!' In the *Tasks of the Proletariat in the Present Revolution*, Lenin's writing had very much the flavour of permanent revolution: 'The specific feature of the present situation in Russia is that the country is *passing* from the first stage of the revolution – which, owing to the insufficient class-consciousness and organisation of the proletariat, placed power in the hands of the bourgeoisie – to its *second* stage, which must place power in the hands of the proletariat and the poorest sections of the peasants' (*SW2*: 30). In August and September 1917, Lenin again turns to the analogy of the Paris Commune of 1871. But unlike his conclusions of 1905, which emphasised the muddled class basis of the Commune, he examines its experience in relation to the technique of seizing political power: Lenin calls for the smashing of the state machine and the election of all officials and he calls for an alliance of workers and peasants to break up the 'bureaucratic military state machine' (*State and Revolution*, *SW2*: 265–6).

The social base of the 'dictatorship of the proletariat' could rest 'only on a definite class, namely, the urban workers and the factory, industrial workers in general, [only this class] is able to lead the whole mass of the working and exploited people in the struggle to throw off the yoke of capital, in actually carrying it out, in the struggle to maintain and consolidate the victory, in the work of creating the new, socialist social system and in the entire struggle for the complete abolition of classes' (*A Great Beginning*, *SW3*: 173).

Here then we have a clear adaptation of Marxist historical materialism to feudal-type regimes undergoing capitalist development. The full stage of capitalist development may be skipped under certain circumstances. Marx, in *The German Ideology*, pointed out that colonised countries (he had America in mind) establish the 'most advanced form of intercourse' derived from their conquerors (Marx 1968: 91). Likewise, as Germany and Britain did not go through the stage of slavery, Russia was now destined, in Lenin's view, to miss out processing through the capitalist stage. The awareness of these political goals and the assumptions on which he made them is paramount to the understanding of Lenin's thought. The imperialist character of monopoly capitalism had not only set capitalism in motion in Russia without a significant indigenous bourgeoisie, but it had resulted in a horrendous capitalist war in Europe which had, Lenin believed, brought the European working class to the verge of revolution. Lenin now adopted in effect Trotsky's earlier analysis of uninterrupted revolution. Both thinkers came to justify seizing power in Russia on the assumption that it was the first step of a world-wide proletarian revolution. Unlike Trotsky, however, Lenin had already developed a theory of Party organisation and leadership of the revolution. His political theory is one of political action: the Party, to which we turn next, is a crucial element and instrument of political action – it cannot be divorced from Lenin's political goals. Both his views on the organisation of revolutionary forces and the world context of Tsarist Russia in the early twentieth century have to be seen as interrelated components of Lenin's world view and not to be studied out of context, divorced from their theoretical and historical conjunction.

THE ORGANISATIONAL THEORY OF THE PARTY

Marx and Engels were principally concerned with the anatomy and dynamics of capitalism. While they both believed that inherent laws governing the system would lead to the victory of the proletariat, they said very little about the tactics of the struggle, they provided no interpretation of the ways that the proletariat had to be organised or the kind of alliances which had to be arranged for the working class to become a ruling class. Lenin, however, was particularly concerned with these questions and with the political organisation of the proletariat in Russia. His *Development of Capitalism in Russia* was a Marxist interpretation of the evolution of capitalism, and his pamphlet *What is to be Done?* (1902) provided the tactics for Russian social-democracy in its struggle with the autocracy. In short, Lenin argued that a particular form of organisation is necessary for a revolutionary party to secure the interest of the proletariat under the conditions it faced in Russia. In *The State and Revolution* (completed August 1917, published 1918), Lenin turned to consider the leadership of the proletariat and other classes after the socialist revolution had taken place. Here Lenin discussed the role of the masses in the revolution and in the subsequent proletarian state – 'the revolutionary dictatorship of the proletariat' – and he looked forward to the process of administration which would ideally take place under socialism considered in the long term. Both these texts are important components of Lenin's world view and both texts again mark a departure from orthodox Marxist thought.

Lenin's development of Marxism, particularly in *What is to be Done?* lay in his emphasis on the importance of organisation. Lenin adopts a Weberian type of attitude in stressing the importance of organisational structures, and he welds this viewpoint to a Marxian analysis of class. Weber emphasised the importance of 'bureaucratic' structures which he saw as the dominant tendency of the development of industrial society. But Weber had an ambiguous attitude towards the bureaucratic process. Large bureaucratic organisations promote 'rational efficiency, continuity of operation, speed, precision, and calculation of results'. Rational organisation 'compels modern man to become a specialised expert' (Gerth and Mills: 49). Politically, however, Weber feared the bureaucratic process. He saw it as being antithetical to democracy, to the independence of the individual and a challenge to freedom: 'rationality . . . is seen as adverse to personal freedom'. Bureaucracy is a shackle on the freedom of the individual. 'The dictatorship of the official and not that of the worker is on the march' (*ibid.*). For Weber, the evolution of 'efficient bureaucracies' led to 'a new iron cage of serfdom' (Mommsen 1974: 57). Under socialism, the need for bureaucratic organisations would increase: 'Socialism would . . . . require a still higher degree of formal bureaucratisation than capitalism' (Weber 1947: 339).

This was not so for Lenin, who stresses the utilisation and application of organisation, based on hierarchy and specialisation of activity, as a form of decision-making by the workers' movement. Capitalism, argues Lenin, provides the *'pre-conditions* that *enable* [everyone] . . . to take part in the administration of the State' (*State and Revolution, SW2:* Ch. V, §4). Hence Lenin stands almost alone as a Marxist in considering the administrative or bureaucratic process as part of the establishment of a socialist system. This is implicit in Lenin's theory of Party organisation. In *State and Revolution,* Lenin discusses the forms the organisation of things may take in a socialist society – after the withering away of the State. But there is no formal or explicit theory of decision-making in Lenin's work (as in that of sociologists such as Weber); organisation is part of Lenin's revolutionary praxis and is discussed in the context of the practical activity of the workers' movement.

In *What is to be Done?* Lenin put forward two criticisms of the ways in which the workers' movement was developing in Russia. He saw great dangers involved in the growth of trade unionism and 'spontaneity' among the working class. He feared that these developments would detract from a revolutionary leadership and consciousness of the proletariat. While Marx and Engels in the *Communist Manifesto* recognised the importance of combinations of workers which help to unite them as a class, they also pointed to the divisions between groups of workers. Engels was particularly aware of the segmental and narrow aims of groups of workers expressed through their unions. 'The [British] trade unions exclude on principle, and by virtue of their statutes, all political action and consequently also participation in the general activity of the working class as a class' (Engels, letter to Bernstein, 17 June 1879, cited in Hyman 1971:10). Lenin developed this pessimisitc attitude of Engels in his analysis of trade unionism as a whole. He recognised that it did have some positive aspects in helping to unite the working class, but trade unionism might detract the working class away from revolutionary activity. Trade union activity was organised on the basis of a trade or craft and therefore it divided the working class into strata or segments which worked against the formation of class consciousness. Also it encouraged workers to consider their short-term goals (which might possibly be at the expense of other workers). Lenin argued that trade unionism assumes that workers' conditions may be improved within the parameters of a given social order, whereas Marxism calls for the abolition of capitalism, and for the creation of a different socialist social order. Essentially, the trade union struggle was an economistic struggle geared to *improve* conditions of labour (and pay), it was a form of bourgeois, rather than socialist, politics. This does not mean that unions were unimportant but rather that their focus was too narrow, too 'economistic' and they could not alone lead to any major improvement in the conditions of the working class as a whole (see Hammond 1957).

The second component to Lenin's criticisms of the ways that the workers' movement was developing was concerned with its 'spontaneity'. This was particularly important under the conditions of an autocratic police state. The unco-ordinated strikes, elemental uprisings against the factory management led to easy capture by the police and to the removal of the workers' leaders. Lenin argued that Russian socialdemocracy was developing along the lines of an 'organisation of workers'. Here again Lenin was to oppose the Mensheviks who had in mind the model of the large European socialist parties, particularly that of Germany. In absolutist Russia a quite different form of organisation was apposite (*What is to be Done? SW*1: 178).

Lenin's recommendations were of two kinds. The first concerned the conditions for party membership and the second was about the way that decisions should be made in the party. The Party was to be 'an organisation of revolutionaries which must consist first and foremost of people whose profession is that of a revolutionary'. Unlike a workers' organisation which was to be as 'broad as possible', organisations of revolutionary Social-Democrats must 'of necessity be not too extensive and as secret as possible' (*ibid.*). Lenin emphasised the condition of being a revolutionary in a Marxist sense, of adopting a revolutionary perspective, of viewing Russian development in terms of class conflict and of bringing about the eventual triumph of the working class. Lenin was particularly concerned that the Party identify with the working class as a whole as a movement in history. He rejected forms of definition of the working class which counterposed the interests of manual and non-manual groups of workers – and which was implicit in the views of many trade unions. He called for 'all distinctions between workers and intellectuals to be obliterated'. For Lenin, the prime consideration was the identity of a person with the working class.

Indeed, socialist intellectuals play an important role in bringing 'theory' to manual workers: ideas which explain their social position and their role in history to them. The tasks of professional revolutionaries were to infuse a Marxist *weltanschauung* and Marxist policies into the working class. Lenin realised that a socialist consciousness had to be informed by an awareness of Marxist theory and the latter could not be spontaneously created by the working class. Theory influences practice: there can be no revolutionary practice without revolutionary theory. 'The history of all countries shows that the working class, exclusively by its own effort, is able to develop only trade-union consciousness, i.e. the conviction that it is necessary to combine in unions, fight the employers, and strive to compel the government to pass necessary labour legislation' (*What is to be Done? SW*1: 144). The Party, through professional revolutionaries, had to bring Marxist ideas to the working class. 'Class political consciousness can be brought to the workers *only from outside*. That is, only from outside the economic struggle, from outside the sphere of relations between workers and employers' (*ibid.*: 152). While Lenin is often criticised in the West for intellectual elitism, it is true that Plekhanov, Akselrod and Kautsky had also noted that the intelligentsia had a role of communicating socialist ideas to the proletariat and that a *socialist* consciousness would not arise spontaneously (see discussion in Harding 1977: 167–8 and Parkin 1979: 151–2). Lenin anticipates many contemporary Marxists who emphasise the domination of bourgeois ideological constraints binding the working class to capitalism. He saw the Party as being made up of persons who were 'class conscious' in the sense indicated above. In Russian conditions, he did not favour a widely recruited trade-union type of socialist party though it would be wrong to conclude that Lenin wanted a small conspiratorial type of party at all times. The Party was intended to draw into its activity the wider masses.

It must be emphasised that *What is to be Done?* was concerned with the Russia of 1902, with a struggle for founding a political party of revolutionaries under the difficult conditions of the Tsarist dictatorship. The 'trade union' struggle known to Lenin was indeed a very narrow one. Even in this work he makes clear that an organisation of professional revolutionaries would make it possible for a *'greater . . .* number of people from the working class and from other social classes . . . to join the movement and perform active work in it' (*What is to be Done? SW1:* 188). During the 1905 Revolution, conditions were such as to allow for a considerable widening of the Party organisation. In November 1905, Lenin recognised that conditions had radically changed, making outdated some of his earlier proposals: he called for a widening of Party membership and said that 'the working class is instinctively spontaneously social-democratic and more than ten years of work put in by social-democracy has done a great deal to transform this spontaneity into consciousness' (*The Reorganisation of the Party, CW10:* 32). But, unlike the Mensheviks, the Bolsheviks did not this time undertake an extensive organisation of trade unions and they kept the secret apparatus of the Party intact. Lenin wanted to preserve the Marxist nature of the Party in the sense that it stood for the cause of the proletariat to be achieved by revolutionary means: this could be ensured by restricting leadership to Marxists. As Lukacs (1971: 73) has noted, Lenin was concerned with the *steps* that are necessary to move towards socialism. The Party was to be a 'vanguard' of the proletariat. It was to decide what should be the correct strategy for the liberation of the working class. To be charitable to Lenin, this does not mean that the Party should manipulate the working class, but that the Party, being guided by Marxist theory, should be able to channel the activity of the working class towards revolution and thereby to socialism. It articulated, in Rousseau's terms, the general will of the proletariat. In *State and Revolution* Lenin speaks of the Party as 'the vanguard of the proletariat [which is] capable of assuming power and of *leading the whole people* to socialism, of directing and organising the new order, of being the teacher, the guide, the leader of all the working and exploited people in organising their social life without the bourgeoisie and against the bourgeoisie' (*SW2*: 255). The role of the Party then was not only paramount in leading the forces of revolution, but was also to be hegemonic in the construction of socialism.

The second recommendation of Lenin about party organisation was concerned with the process of decision-making in the Party. Decisions should be taken and enforced according to the principle of 'democratic centralism'. Lenin stresses the need for centralised control of the Party. In *What is to be Done?* he argued that the principle of ' "broad democracy" in Party organisation . . . is nothing more than a *useless and harmful toy*. It is a useless toy because, as a matter of fact, no revolutionary organis- ation has ever practised, or could practise, *broad* democracy. . . . It is harmful because any attempt to practise the "broad democratic princi- ples" will simply facilitate the work of the police in carrying out large- scale raids, it will perpetuate the prevailing amateurishness, divert the thoughts of the practical workers from the serious and imperative tasks of training themselves to become professional revolutionaries to that of drawing up detailed "paper" rules for election systems' (*SW1*: 200).

It was in 1906 that Lenin declared that 'the principle of democratic centralism [in the Party is now] universally recognised' (*A Tactical Plat- form for the Unity Congress of the RSDLP*, *CW10*: 163). By 'democratic' Lenin understood that decisions should be resolved according to major- ity vote of the central committee (of the executive) of the Party and that all Party members had the right to participate in general Party policy- making. The Party Congress was to be supreme over policy. There were to be periodic elections of the leading officers of the Party. 'Democratic' has to be interpreted in the context of a collectivist membership united over the goals of revolutionary Marxism. In the event of disagreement over tactics, or policy, an attempt is made to reach a compromise.

By 'centralism', Lenin meant that once general policy was agreed, the day-to-day operation of the Party had to be decided centrally, where all information and the Party leadership are located, and the de- cisions of central bodies were absolutely binding on lower bodies. In Lenin's view, democratic centralism was a synthesis between demo- cracy and central control: it gave members the right to participation and it gave a creative role for the leadership. Democratic centralism was the formula for the creation of a political party of a new type. Lenin's views on centralisation have been distorted by some writers who stress the 'command' element in Lenin's thought. Meyer, for instance, cites the following statement by Lenin:

Marxist criticisms of Lenin's views on organisation

The Party is in a position in which the strictest centralisation and the most stringent discipline are absolute necessities. All decisions of higher headquarters are absolutely binding for the lower. Every decision must first of all be executed, and only after that an appeal to the corresponding Party organ is permissible. In this sense, outright military discipline is indispensable in the party at the present time. (*Protokoly VIII Sézda RKP (b)* p.414, cited by Meyer 1957: 99.)

This statement, however, was written at the time of the Eighth Party Congress in March 1919 when the Party was involved in fighting the Civil War and should not be taken as a general law of Party organisation for all time.

We shall consider below (pp. 56–61) Lenin's ideas on participation in the State; it is worthwhile noting, however, that he did not exclude 'autonomy and federation' under democratic centralism as a method of organisation. Under *socialism*, initiative and inventiveness had to come from below (original version of *Immediate Tasks*, CW27: 207–9; see also Harding 1980: Chapter 8).

Whatever may be said about Lenin's opportunism, his theory of Party organisation did provide leadership of the revolutionary forces in 1917. Contrasted to Trotsky, who had advocated a revolutionary upheaval by the masses, but relied on spontaneity to carry it out, Lenin conceived of the instrument for the leadership of such an uprising.

MARXIST CRITICISMS OF
LENIN'S VIEWS ON ORGANISATION

Lenin's views have also not been received with anything like universal acclaim by Marxists. He has been criticised by some as having corrupted Marxism: they have argued that he lacked faith in the revolutionary potential and creativity of the working class. Many such writers have based their case on the dictum expressed in the *General Rules of the International Working Men's Association* (1864, English version 1874), that 'the emancipation of the working classes must be conquered by the working classes themselves' (*SW1*: 386). It is claimed that a centralised form of Party leadership, therefore, is a distortion and revision of Marxism; and the Russian Social-Democratic Labour Party itself split into Bolsheviks and Mensheviks over this and other issues. This principle of organisation is still a major difference between European social-democratic parties and communist ones – though this is becoming less so in the era of Eurocommunism. The Mensheviks and those like them wanted a wider membership to include socialist trade unionists who would not necessarily be either active or Marxist. The Mensheviks also sought greater powers for local party organisations, they opposed strong central control and advocated that local secretaries be elected in the locality, if this was possible. The Bolsheviks, in line with Lenin's view, favoured firm central control and the appointment of all leading cadres, including those at local levels. The essence of the Bolshevik/Menshevik split was that Lenin opposed a 'loose, amorphous body of occasional sympathisers' and sought a 'Party of activists, of cadres, which aims . . . to assemble a class-conscious proletarian vanguard' (Geras 1977: 5).

Harding has reminded us that Lenin shared many of the views of other leading Russian social-democrats, such as Akselrod and Plekhanov (1977: Chapter 7). One should not minimise, however, the opposition, in principle, by some Russian Marxists to Lenin's strategies. Even if Lenin's co-editors in *Iskra* had accepted his views between 1899 and 1902, this does not mean that one can say without important qualification that Lenin was the expression of 'The orthodoxy of Russian Marxism' (Harding 1977: 187). Unlike Harding, I would attribute Lenin's 'orthodoxy' not so much to Marxist antecedents, as to that of the Russian revolutionary tradition. Lenin was the heir of the Populists; he had been strongly influenced by their ideas on political organisation and it was not by chance that he adopted the title of Chernyshevsky's book, *What is to be Done?* for his treatise on party organisation. Tkachev followed Chernyshevsky in emphasising the role of intellectuals in bringing 'consciousness' to the masses and he added the idea of a disciplined and centralised political party: the Bolsheviks were drawing on an important component of *Russian* rather than social-democratic revolutionary political culture.* This was not the case, for instance, for the Jews in Russia whose socialists adopted the Western political tradition and the German form of social-democratic organisation (Brym 1978: 89). The Mensheviks also, being far less Russian in composition, were also more trade-union oriented and more committed to the German model. Lenin was certainly opposed by many Russian Marxists of the time: Trotsky and Parvus had quite a different outlook, as did Luxemburg. Harding ignores the fact that the editorial board of *Iskra* was divided into 'hards' and 'softs' (for and against Lenin) even before the 1903 Conference. (See *Leninski sbornik*: vol. xi, 309.) While the wording of the form of party organisation which initially led to the split between

---

* For an interesting discussion of the relationship between the values of Nechaev, Lenin and Stalin, see Pomper (1978).

Mensheviks and Bolsheviks was superficially not very different, it was of great significance. For, as Haimson (1955: 175) has noted, the Menshevik version was copied from the statutes of the German Social-Democratic Party, whereas Lenin's version (as did his view of the Party) emphasised more the place of the active committed Marxist. Following 1903, the lines of division became deeper and were manifested not only in organisation, but also in tactics and objectives.

Perhaps the best-known criticisms of Lenin's theory of the Party have been put by Trotsky and Rosa Luxemburg in their polemics with Lenin before the October Revolution. Trotsky then regarded Lenin's centralism as leading to a dictatorship over the Party and over the proletariat. In 1905, Trotsky looked to the self-activity of the working class as the prime actor in the revolutionary process: 'The Russian proletariat was an independent, vital revolutionary force, both in the sense of its economic-based political strength as well as that of its conscientiousness, idealism and devotion to socialist goals' (Knei-Paz: 171). In *Our Political Tasks*, Trotsky opposes Lenin in principle. He argues that the Party envisaged by Lenin would not be one of co-ordinating the working class, but it would lead to the substitution of the Party for the class and to the substitution of the professionals of the Party for the Party itself. By 1917, however, Trotsky had changed his theoretical line and recognised what Knei-Paz terms 'the indispensability of the revolutionary elite – the 'vanguard', the 'leaders', the 'very idea of a Party' (Knei-Paz 1978: 228).

Luxemburg (1961) spelled out in some detail her criticisms of Lenin's theory. She asserted that Lenin's principles of centralism rest on the 'blind subordination ... of all party organs to the centre' and on the 'rigorous separation of the organised nucleus of revolutionaries from its social-revolutionary surroundings' (1961: 88). She accuses Lenin of restricting the 'revolutionary initiative' of the masses. 'The ultra-centralism asked [for] by Lenin is full of the sterile spirit of the overseer. It is not a positive and creative spirit. *Lenin's concern is not so much to make the activity of the party more fruitful as to control the party – to narrow the movement rather than to develop it, to bind rather than to unify it' (ibid.: 94). Luxemburg also saw Lenin's theory as giving undue influence to intellectuals as such over the working class. 'Nothing will more surely enslave a young labor movement to an intellectual elite hungry for power than this bureaucratic straight-jacket, which will immobilize the movement and turn it into an automaton manipulated by a Central Committee' (ibid.: 102). Luxemburg for her part stressed the conditions necessary for the realisation of social-democracy's goals as lying with the existence of 'a large contingent of workers educated in the political struggle' and with 'the possibility for the workers to develop their own political activity through direct influence on public life, in a party press, and public congresses, etc.' (*ibid.*: 89).

It seems to me that Luxemburg's criticisms of Lenin are one-sided and unfair. She takes as an example the advanced states of Western Europe and ignores the real problems of organisation in Russia. In *What is to be Done?* Lenin did stress the centralisation of Party control which was necessary to maintain the integrity of the Party under Tsarist conditions. Here, as we have seen, Lenin was concerned with forming an organisation which could mobilise the masses. In other places, he said that participation had to be encouraged. Lenin in 1907 made it clear that the ideas of *What is to be Done?* had to be read in the context of the time. 'The basic mistake made by those who now criticise *What is to be Done?* is to treat the pamphlet apart from its connection with the concrete historical situation of a definite, and now long past, period in the development of our Party' (Preface to the collection, *Twelve Years*, CW13: 101, cited by Harding 1977: 161).

In *State and Revolution* (discussed below) there is much more emphasis on the relationship of political leadership to popular participation. This work has been widely regarded as a minor aberration in, and deviation from, Lenin's centralist and authoritarian viewpoint (see Barfield 1971, Daniels 1953). There seems to be no justification for this position, if its relevance is to be seen as Lenin's ideals of what a socialist state *should* be like. Lenin had a belief that in the proper environment the working class would come to realise its class interest. In *What is to be Done?* the Party is considered to be necessary to articulate the interest of the working class. In *State and Revolution*, we have a clearer picture of Lenin's optimistic view of human nature, of how the masses, if the conditions were right, would develop under socialism after the revolution. Marxists, it should be remembered, believe in the ultimate perfectibility of man; in this work, we see Lenin's 'fundamental philosophy of man, his inner convictions of human nature, his ideals for a more humane world' (Barfield 1971: 56).

One must also bear in mind that in 1917 Lenin was confronted by a situation of dual power in the form of the Soviets and the Provisional Government. He also brought out, in the months immediately following October, the participatory role of the masses in the Soviets. His tactics were to channel activity away from the Provisional Government and therefore he emphasised the revolutionary potential of the Soviets and the ways they could include the revolutionary masses. In this respect Lenin now appeared to converge to Trotsky's ideas on participation, on the more spontaneous role of the masses, which he had outlined in 1905.

PARTY AND SOVIETS

One should not, however, assume that Lenin idealised spontaneous forms of participation in the Soviets without qualification. Liebman, for instance, remarks that 'it is a fact, and one of the highest importance, that the "role of the Party" is practically absent from the great social and political project that Lenin drew up on the eve of the conquest of power [i.e. *State and Revolution*]' (Liebman 1975: 198–9). Kolakowski also takes a similar view: in contrast to Lenin's earlier writings, he argues, *State and Revolution* 'says nothing whatever about the party' (1978: vol. 2, 501). But as we saw above (pp. 47–8), Lenin does give the Party an important role in this tract: it is one of being 'teacher', 'guide' and 'leader'. To argue that Lenin regarded the Soviets as representing some form of pristine democracy, not requiring the control and leadership of the Party (see Liebman: 198) shows a complete misunderstanding of Lenin's theory, strategy and tactics. When the Soviets first appeared in 1905, and in contradistinction to those Party activists in Russia who sought to ignore the Soviets (as they were not composed of Marxists) in favour of the Party, Lenin argued that Party and Soviets were complementary and coined the slogan: 'Both Party and Soviets' (see Lane 1975: 88). The Soviets were expressive organs, the task of the Party was to provide them with political leadership. In *'Left-Wing' Communism – An Infantile Disorder*, Lenin makes clear the relationship between the Party and the masses:

In Russia today, the connection between leaders, party, class and masses, as well as the attitude of the dictatorship of the proletariat and its party to the trade unions, are concretely as follows: the dictatorship of the proletariat is exercised by the proletariat organised in the Soviets; the proletariat is guided by the Communist Party of Bolsheviks. . . . No important political or organisational question is decided by any state institution in our republic without the guidance of the Party's Central Committee. (*SW3*: 316–17)

And he goes on to add that 'all the work of the Party is carried on through the Soviets' (*ibid.*: 318). In 1919 Lenin rounds on those who opposed the 'dictatorship of one party': 'Yes, the dictatorship of the Party! We stand for it and cannot depart from this ground, since this is the Party which in the course of decades has won for itself the position of vanguard of the factory industrial proletariat' (cited in Carr: vol. 1, 236). And in *The Trade Unions, the Present Situation and Trotsky's Mistakes*, Lenin says that the Party 'absorbs the vanguard of the proletariat and this vanguard exercises the dictatorship of the proletariat' (*CW32*: 20).

The Bolshevik counter-argument to those who say that they lack faith in the development of a revolutionary consciousness of the working class is to argue that the Leninist line is not to counterpose the Party against the consciousness of the working class, but to point out that the role of the Party is to provide the *leadership* by which the working class will realise its class consciousness. For Lenin, Marxist analysis establishes the *objective* conditions of the working class; the Party provides leadership: it cannot legitimately substitute itself for the working class.

Marx and Engels also considered the importance of ideological leadership. In the *Communist Manifesto*, Marx and Engels recognised that 'entire sections of the ruling classes are ... precipitated into the proletariat, or are at least threatened in their conditions of existence. These also supply the proletariat with fresh elements of enlightenment and progress' (Marx-Engels, *SW1*: 43). Marx and Engels pointed out that the workers, as they gain class consciousness, become organised into 'a political party' (*ibid.*: 43). But while one may point to antecedents in the writings of Marx and Engels, it seems to me that these thinkers did not have in mind the conditions of Tsarist Russia, and the kind of Party that Lenin was advocating. Marx and Engels, also, in line with their more orthodox followers, had a belief that as the contradictions of capitalism developed, the political consciousness of the working class would parallel or reflect these changes and that a revolutionary consciousness, aided perhaps by intellectuals such as themselves, would grow. One should admit, I think, that this did not, and has not, happened. Within advanced capitalist states mass working-class politics have largely been 'bourgeois' politics. Lenin recognised this tendency and provided an alternative strategy.

THE ROLE OF THE STATE

Lenin's was not only a strategy for the political organisation of revolutionary forces, but also an analysis of the political power of the ruling class, expressed through the state. His writings in *State and Revolution* are of considerable importance in this context. In this tract there are two major themes. First, Lenin discusses the activity of the state as a weapon of struggle used by the proletariat against hostile class forces: the state was to be the actuality of 'the dictatorship of the proletariat'. Second, Lenin seeks to describe the form of organisation and the participatory process which would characterise socialist society. There is then a sequence of stages. The socialist revolution would abolish the *bourgeois* state, which would be replaced by the *proletarian* state (*State and Revolution*, CW 25: 397), which in turn would, with the consolidation of the revolution, begin to wither away.

The essence of the Russian state confronting the proletariat was that it was 'a social organisation of force: the state is an organisation of violence for the suppression of some class' (*ibid.*: 402). Here Lenin is following in the footsteps of Marx who, in the *Critique of the Gotha Program*, said that in the period of the transition from capitalism to socialism 'The state can be nothing but *the revolutionary dictatorship of the proletariat*' (SW2: 30). As such the Tsarist state had to be abolished by force. Lenin, then, focusses on its repressive institutions, and the need for physical force to overcome them. The place of the Tsarist state would be taken by the dictatorship of the proletariat. The working class had to form its own state apparatus. 'A Marxist is someone who *extends* the recognition of the class struggle to the recognition of the *dictatorship of the proletariat*' (CW25: 412). (For a more detailed discussion of this point see Liebman 1975: 190–5.) The proletarian state would be the 'proletariat organised as the ruling class' (CW25: 402). As Lenin put it: 'The theory of the class struggle, applied by Marx to the question of the state and the socialist revolution, leads as a matter of course to the recognition of the *political rule* of the proletariat, of its dictatorship, i.e. of individual power directly backed by the armed force of the people. The overthrow of the bourgeoisie can only be achieved by the proletariat becoming the *ruling class*, capable of crushing the inevitable and desperate resistance of the bourgeoisie and of organising *all* the working and exploited people for the new economic system.'

'The proletariat needs state power, a centralised organisation of force, an organisation of violence, both to crush the resistance of the exploiters and to lead the enormous mass of the population – the peasants, the petty bourgeoisie, and semi-proletarians – in the work of organising a socialist economy' (*ibid.*: 404). There are then two tasks for the socialist state in the early period of power: a political one of crushing the bourgeoisie and an administrative one of organising a socialist economy. Lenin believed that the fall of the autocracy would not come about by the powers of reason, or persuasion through democratic means, or through the electoral process giving control of the bourgeois state – the state was based on force, and force would have to be used to destroy class rule. Lenin was quite adamant on the fact that for an *ascendant* class to achieve political power, a dictatorship was necessary (see *Theses and Report on Bourgeois Democracy*, CW28: 458). The ruling class would have to be dispossessed by force. The dictatorship of the proletariat would also, at least in the short run, also rest on force: 'The revolutionary dictatorship of the proletariat is rule won and maintained by the use of violence by the proletariat against the bourgeoisie, rule that is unrestricted by any laws' (*The Proletarian Revolution and the Renegade Kautsky*, CW28: 236; for further discussion of this point, see Balibar 1977: Chapter 3). Lenin justified the use of terror, as a reserve. Even during the new economic policy following the Revolution, Lenin wrote to Kamenev that 'we shall again have recourse to terror and to economic terror' (cited by Lewin 1973: 133). As the Party represented in an 'objective' sense the interests of the proletariat, so the dictatorship of the proletariat *correctly* expresses the interests of the *entire mass* of working and exploited people, all semi-proletarians ... all small peasants and similar categories' (*Draft of RCP's Reply to Ind. S-D of Germany*, CW30: 338). On the one side of Lenin's attitude to political power is the role of leadership, on the other is popular participation.

The Soviets were instruments to be used both against the bourgeoisie and to aggregate the interests of the non-bourgeois, though not necessarily Marxist, popular forces. In the latter respect we see the other side of Lenin, one that places emphasis on the participation of the masses in the revolution and in socialist society. Popular activity was to be channelled into revolutionary action by the Soviets led by the Party. Here we have an example of Lenin's ability to innovate. Unlike many Bolsheviks in Russia in 1905, Lenin saw the potential of the Soviets, which spontaneously arose in that year. They were not assemblies of Marxist socialdemocrats, but revolutionary strike committees made up of a wide spectrum of political interests. Lenin's tactics were to utilise these 'nonparty' bodies to mobilise under the Party the wider masses into the revolutionary struggle. Led by the Party, the Soviets were used, in Lukacs's words: 'to overcome by education the inertia and the fragmentation of these strata and *to train them for active and independent participation in the life of the state*' (1970: 67).

Lenin's opposition to 'bureaucracy' is not something new to be found in his essay *Better Fewer, but Better,* written in March 1923, arising out of the experience of revolution; this is a restatement of the dangers of bureaucracy as Lenin saw them even before the Revolution. Lenin had a belief, summed up by Lewin (1973: 123–4), that the quality of administration depended on the quality of the 'senior cadres'. If the senior cadres were steeped in 'bureaucratic attitudes' this was something inherited from the previous regime, from its low level of culture. This argument is used by many of Lenin's successors (as we shall see below) to explain the degeneration of bureaucracy under Stalin. Lenin, however, assumed that professionals and administrators would act in an altruistic way – if their politics were right, if they identified with Bolshevik power. He did not contemplate the fact that specialised knowledge itself may be a form of domination over the citizen.

Socialist society, Lenin believed, should not be characterised by similar forms of domination as in the bourgeois state. He strongly advocated direct participation by the masses in administration. What he aspired to was a system under which 'much of "primitive" democracy will inevitably be revived since, for the first time in the history of civilised society, the *mass* of the population will rise to taking an *independent* part, not only in voting and elections, *but also in the everyday administration of the state.* Under socialism *all* will govern in turn and will soon become accustomed to no one governing' (*The State and Revolution, SW* 2: 323–4). Lenin makes it clear that 'Revolution consists in the proletariat destroying the "administrative apparatus" and the whole state machine', but he emphasises that, during the 'dictatorship of the proletariat' the state itself would continue, and the old state machine would be replaced 'by a new one, made up of the armed workers'. Revolution consists of the new class 'commanding and governing with the aid of a new machine'. The importance of organisation is brought out by Lenin when, discussing large-scale industry, he points out that 'The technique of all these enterprises makes absolutely imperative the strictest discipline, the utmost precision on the part of everyone in carrying out his allotted task for otherwise the whole enterprise may come to a stop, or the finished product may be damaged' (*ibid.*: 318, see also Lane 1974 and Wright 1978).

A parallel may be drawn between Lenin's views on capitalism and bureaucracy, on the one hand, and industrialism and management, on the other. While Lenin opposed bureaucracy because of its oppressive class character, management he regarded as necessary in an industrial system, and capitalism, he believed, had devised advanced forms of organisation. He likens a socialist economic system to the postal service: 'once we have overthrown the capitalists . . . and smashed the bureaucratic machine of the modern state . . . we shall have a splendidly equipped mechanism which can very well be set going by the united workers themselves. . . . Our immediate aim is to organise the whole economy on the lines of the postal service so that the technicians, foremen and accountants, as well as all officials, shall receive salaries no higher than "a working-man's wages", and under the control and leadership of the armed proletariat' (*State and Revolution, SW2*: 273–4).

In other words, with the abolition of class interests (presided over by the party) the regular administration of things would begin to replace coercion and manipulation of people, and wage differentials would fall. In this much used quotation we have a reference to Lenin's egalitarianism. It should be made clear, however, that equality of remuneration did not figure prominently in Lenin's social philosophy. In this respect Lenin followed Marx, who had made it explicit that 'it was in general a mistake to fuss about so-called *distribution* and put the principal stress on it. . . . Vulgar socialism (and from it in turn a section of the democracy) has taken over from the bourgeois economists the consideration and treatment of distribution as independent of the mode of production and hence the presentation of socialism as turning principally on distribution' (*Critique of the Gotha Program, SW* 2: 23–4). Engels in a letter to Bebel criticises the phrase in the Gotha Program concerning the 'elimination of all social and political inequality' instead of 'the abolition of all class distinctions', and he goes on to point out that 'there will always exist a *certain* degree of inequality' (*Critique, SW2*: 39). Lenin viewed idleness, the exploitation of labour by a propertied class, as immoral; he took for granted that once the major *class*-determined form of privilege had been abolished, other forms of inequality would be either unimportant or would, with time, wither away as socialist consciousness developed. Lenin made it clear that 'General talk about freedom, equality and democracy is in fact but a blind repetition of concepts shaped by the relations of commodity production. . . . Long ago Engels in his Anti-Dühring explained that the concept of "equality" is moulded from the relations of commodity production; equality becomes a prejudice if it is not understood to mean the *abolition of classes*. This elementary truth regarding the distinction between the bourgeois-democratic and the socialist conception of equality is constantly being forgotten' (*Economics and Politics, CW30*: 116–17). Here we see a major difference from other forms of Western social-democracy, whose philosophy and ideology is strongly steeped in distributional concepts of equality. Lenin defined socialism as 'the abolition of commodity economy' (*The Agrarian Question, CW* 15: 138), and the foundations of capitalism he saw as 'the power of money, commodity production and the domination of the market' (*Campaign for the Elections to the Fourth Duma, CW*17: 381). (See also below pp. 70–73.)

In Lenin's view, centralised direction and control were not to be authoritarian and dictatorial: he strongly advocated direct participation by the masses in administration and his views on participation in *State and Revolution* have been summarised above. In the *Immediate Tasks of Soviet Power* (28 April 1918), Lenin defines one of the principal character-istics of proletarian democracy as 'the people themselves determine the order and time of elections and are completely free to recall any elected person' (*CW* 27: 272). In *'How to Organise Competition'*, Lenin wrote that 'one of the most important tasks today, if not the most important, is to develop this independent initiative of the workers, and of all the working and exploited peoples generally to develop it as widely as pos-sible in creative *organisational* work' (*SW*2: 469). He saw socialism as an economic and moral form of society superior to capitalism and he also subscribed to idealistic, participatory, and egalitarian values. These were not, however, formulated into a moral philosophy. Barfield points out that Lenin's ideals and his faith in the masses are often ignored in western writings on Lenin (Barfield 1971: 45–56). Lenin's moral philo-sophy was not developed because he believed that ethics was derived from a system of economy. The revolution, Lenin believed, would elim-inate antagonism between classes and the state would begin to 'wither away'. Adam Ulam has emphasised this anarchistic component in Lenin's thought and has argued that the appeal of Marxism in countries at a low level of development is a result of 'the essentially anarchist character' of its protest against capitalism (1955: 28).

Lenin, however, at all points very carefully modifies his utopian goals for practical policy purposes; and the views stated above must be inter-preted as ideals rather than actual policy. Shortly after the Revo-lution, the Party programme of 1919 pointed out that 'while aspiring to equality of remuneration for all kinds of labour and to total communism, the Soviet government cannot consider as its task the immediate realisa-tion of this equality at the present moment when only the first steps are being made towards the transition from capitalism to communism' (*K.P.S.S.* 1953: 423). Also, in practice, the withering away of the state would be a protracted process of unknown length, and during the period following the revolution the need for administration and subordination (*SW*2: 273) would continue. Indeed, in contradistinction to the anarchists, and to present-day social-democratic critics, Lenin had always emphasised participation within a framework of central control and subordination of lower bodies to higher ones. He made it clear that 'We are not utopians, we do not "dream" of dispensing *at once* with all administration, with all subordination.... We want socialist revolution with people as they are now, with people who cannot dispense with subordination, control and "foremen and accountants"' (*The State and Revolution, SW*2: 273). Lenin's ideas about participation – in the Soviets and in the industrial enterprise – must be seen in the context of the leading role of the Party, which places severe limits on the conduct of popular participation.

What must be grasped in analysing Lenin's thought is a distinction between what was practical and necessary, given various forms of political and social constraints, and what was desirable and possible under ideal conditions. Lenin took for granted that 'socialism' was desirable; but he did not define its end-state in ideal terms, rather he was concerned with the political strategy that was desirable to bring political power to the working class and its political party. Perhaps most important of all is a fundamental assumption in Lenin's Marxism that the level of the forces of production determines superstructural relations and that, *under the circumstances of Soviet power*, industrial development ranked more highly than democratic procedures. Lenin criticised the idea of 'industrial democracy' as being 'half-baked and theoretically false'. 'Industry is indispensable, democracy is not ... democracy is a category proper only in the political sphere' (*On Trade Unions, CW* 32: 26). A common error perpetuated by commentators on Lenin is to attribute to him the idea of 'workers' control' in a syndicalist sense – i.e. of the workers in a plant having sovereignty over it. This is false. Lenin never saw workers' control as the 'initiation of fundamental decisions relating to production' (see discussion in Bellis 1979: 214–17). In one of the first decrees of Soviet power, Lenin indeed advocated 'workers' control' but this was in the context of industry being under the ownership of the bourgeoisie; it was a 'contradictory and incomplete measure but an essential one' (*Extraordinary 6th All-Russian Congress of Soviets, CW*28: 139). When faced with problems of economic organisation after 1917 the trade unions were seen by Lenin as 'transmission belts', which would link the working masses to the Party leadership: 'the dictatorship of the proletariat cannot be exercised by a mass proletarian organisation' (*Trade Unions, the Present Situation,* CW32: 21). Lenin's response both to the Workers' Opposition and to the revolt at Kronstadt for workers' control was to emphasise the leadership of the Party, the dictatorship of the proletariat, and the role of specialists. Both Lenin and Trotsky emasculated the trade unions as independent sources of political power.

Lenin's views taken as a whole show that he tried to strike a balance between centralised control and popular participation. In the struggle with capitalism and with the Tsarist autocracy a centralised Party organisation was a weapon of struggle; under socialism the Party and state were conceived of as guiding educative forces developing participation in public affairs. Sheer domination by the Party and bureaucratic control hampering popular participation is, as Garaudy has pointed out, 'the very antithesis of Marx and Lenin' (1970: 86). It would be wrong, however, to conceive of Lenin's ideas on participation as analogous to the possessive individualism of bourgeois society in which the individual (voter, consumer) is (at least in theory) decisive.

In practice, Lenin recognised the role of administration in a socialist state. In this context he saw the Soviets, following Marx's views on the Paris Commune, as 'working, not parliamentary, bodies'. (See discussion in Friedgut 1979: 32–41.) Lenin's ideas were much more like those of Rousseau: Party and state should educate citizens in the general will. Proletarian democracy is 'democracy *for* the poor, *for* the people and not democracy *for* the money-bags' (*State and Revolution,* SW2: 302, italics added). Lenin's method is to place the political apparatuses in the context of the mode of production and the dominant class forces. He does not generalise about the 'state' but considers the 'bourgeois state' or, as here, the 'socialist state' (see Wright 1978: 195n). A pivot of Lenin's analysis is that the state cannot be analysed independently of given class forces: in the case of Soviet Russia, he saw the Party and the 'objective interest' of the proletariat shaping the state's activity.

EVALUATION OF LENIN ON ORGANISATION

What then were Lenin's major amendments to Marxism, in so far as his theory of organisation is concerned? First, Lenin invented the idea of a centrally organised Party of 'committed' Marxists who acted as the vanguard of the working class. Second, Lenin brought out the role of intellectuals (and class conscious workers) in bringing Marxist ideas to the working class. He recognised that a *Marxist* class consciousness would not necessarily develop spontaneously among the working class. Third, while political leadership of the working class was central to Lenin's thought, he did not advocate domination over the working class either by the Party or by its leaders. Such domination may have occurred later but it was an unintended consequence: it was not part of Lenin's intentions. It must be emphasised that Lenin's views on organisation should be seen in the context of his political goals, which in turn were related to his version of historical materialism.

Considering *What is to be Done?* against the background of Imperial Russia in 1902, Lenin's analysis was the correct one. It was obvious that 'open' forms of organisation would lead to the arrest of leaders and to the collapse of the embryo social-democratic organisation. It should be noted that the Mensheviks did not oppose Lenin's views on Party organisation until 1903 and, as I have shown elsewhere (Lane 1975), the Mensheviks did not differ very much in organisational *practice* from the Bolsheviks. But they idealised a quite different role for the Party than did Lenin: they did not see it as a hegemonic force leading the bourgeois revolution. After 1903, and particularly during 1905, they became a much looser, more trade-union based party. Lenin, in stressing the importance of centralised organisation, was following a long tradition in Russian revolutionary thought: Populists such as Ogarev, Tkachev and Nechaev had all advocated a secret conspiratorial form of Party organisation in their attempts to evade the police. There was also a tradition of conspiracy in Russian Social-Democracy, as Harding has emphasised. The centralised organisation of professional Marxist revolutionaries attempting to involve the masses in revolutionary activity would seem to be most apposite in societies which are relatively backward politically or economically. But writers, such as Utechin (1960) who also emphasise these organisational similarities, tend to minimise, or even ignore, the quite different goals of Marxists and Populists.

The model of Party organisation outlined by Lenin has not been particularly appropriate in advanced industrial societies in Western Europe, where the working class already has rights of organisation, has participation in Parliaments and relatively large well-organised and often politically activated trade unions. It has encouraged sectarianism and has tended to cut off Marxists from the masses of the working classes organised in trade-union based social-democratic parties. Luxemburg's criticisms are more relevant in this context. Whether we are justified in attributing to Lenin the failure of the Communist parties in Western Europe and the United States, however, is disputable. He strongly condemned ultra-Leftists who idolised the 'Soviets' and 'the dictatorship of the proletariat' (see *'Left-Wing' Communism, SW3*: 322) and who ignored the actual political attitudes of the masses: 'How can one say that "Parliamentarianism is politically obsolete", when "millions" and "legions" of proletarians are not only still in favour of parliamentarianism in general, but are downright "counter-revolutionary"?' Lenin was chiefly concerned with the strategy for revolution in backward autocratic Russia in the early twentieth century. It is doubtful whether Lenin can be held responsible for the bureaucratic trends in the Soviet Party under Stalin after his death, and we shall turn to this problem in Chapter 3.

Again the fact that the Soviet Party during the time of Stalin dominated the world communist parties and the model of the Soviet Party was slavishly copied elsewhere, cannot be held to be the responsibility of Lenin.* (See Garaudy 1970: 84–6.) Lenin's theory of Party organisation, at least as originally conceived, seems to be more relevant to organising the masses under oppressive autocratic conditions (Russia, China, Vietnam) than it does to organising the working class in advanced industrial parliamentary-type societies. His practical political activity in Russia has borne fruit – the Bolsheviks attained power, but his aspirations for a socialist participatory democracy have not been achieved. As Lenin has reminded us: 'It was easy for Russia to *start* a socialist revolution, but it will be more difficult for Russia than for the European countries to *continue* the revolution and bring about its consummation' (*'Left-Wing' Communism, SW3*: 330).

Lenin's praxis was that the revolutionary forces would follow the lead of the Bolsheviks and start a socialist revolution – leadership was essential to turn the latent and inert psychological orientations of the masses into revolutionary consciousness. But it does not follow from this that a socialist transformation could be achieved at one stroke – this is utopianism. As we shall discuss later, Russia was not appropriate for the introduction of fully *socialist* economic, political and administrative relations, because of peculiarly Russian factors inherited by the Revolution: the particular stock of personalities, the level of productive forces and the culture, in a general sense. The seizure of power in October was only the first step in the building of socialism.

---

* It is worthwhile pointing out, however, that the 21 conditions (see E. H. Carr 1966: vol. 3, 197–8) for membership of the Comintern did formulate *political* conditions which distinguished the communist parties from the revisionism of social-democracy. It is also true that Lenin did consider the revolutionary experience of the Russian Party to be of general relevance to the revolutionary struggle in other countries.

POLITICAL SOCIOLOGY OF LENINISM

At this juncture it may be useful to summarise some of the modifications Lenin made to Marxist theory and to itemise some of the major distinctions between Lenin's interpretation of Marxism and those of other non-Leninist Marxists; we may also draw some conclusions about Lenin as a sociologist.

The first major shift in Marxist orientation in Lenin's thinking is that the developing and exploited countries (Russia being the paradigmatic example) have a central place in the theory of socialist revolution. The focus of revolution moved from Western Europe to the East. This was legitimated by the theory of combined or uneven development and of imperialism. This is an integral part of Lenin's thought, it links the socialist revolution in the East to the revolutionary struggles of the Western proletariat: both are interdependent.

In this process the international structure of capitalism was given an important role. In the exploited countries, the class struggle had a national form: the indigenous political elites became more or less integrated into the system of world capitalism, but the toiling masses were exploited on a regional nation-state basis. For Lenin (like the Populists before him) the socialist revolution was carried out by revolutionaries; for Marx and Engels, the emphasis was more exclusively on the workers' movement.

Lenin's methodology sees Marxism as first and foremost a revolutionary class *praxis;* it identifies the social sciences as class sciences. Non-Leninist Marxists shift the emphasis somewhat: they see Marxism as a general approach, as a method; Marx, they say, said that he was not a Marxist, and by this he meant that his own conclusions were modified by history. Much of 'Western Marxism' has been introverted, it has placed interpretation, particularly of culture, at the fore and class action has been a secondary, almost forgotten, topic of concern. Another methodological reaction has been that of the ultra-Leftists of the praxis school who have almost made a fetishism of 'revolutionary action'.

Leninists have viewed their supreme task to be one of the creation of an organisational weapon of the proletariat. The Party has to play a crucial and dominant role in the liberation of the masses. Non-Leninist Marxists, however, have emphasised the spontaneity, the self-development by workers of consciousness. They have tended to emphasise the organic links of the working class with the trade unions, they have stressed such movements as workers' control. Similarly, radicals and socialists have advocated the achievement of equality for various underprivileged groups – more power for manual workers, more rights for women and Blacks, more income for those in poverty. These egalitarian claims play only a very minor role in Lenin's philosophy: the dynamics of world history and the achievement and maintenance of political power of the working class – through the dictatorship of the proletariat – were primary.

Leninists have supported the idea that capitalism may collapse through the snapping of its weakest links, which are located in countries undergoing early industrialisation. The non-Leninist line of argument is that the contradictions of capitalism are greatest in the technically most advanced society. Despite the October Revolution and the rise of other states modelled on the pattern of the USSR, it is argued that socialism will arise first out of the developments in the advanced capitalist states: it is quite utopian to attempt to build socialism in backward underdeveloped societies. This division has led to fundamental differences in the stance of Marxists to the Soviet Union. Leninists have argued that the Soviet bloc represents the dictatorship of the proletariat, and that the countries therein are 'workers' states'. Stalin's interpretation was that on a world scale the class interests of the proletariat should be identified with those of the first socialist state, the Soviet Union. The non-Leninist Marxist, however, argues that the interests of the working class can be decided only by reference to itself: they cannot be identified with the ruling 'working class', or with a Party of that class, in any given state or group of states.

Finally (and here I am anticipating the discussion of the next chapter), after the seizure of power by the Party supported by the working class and other oppressed strata, the previously exploited countries consciously adopt the superior mode of production of the advanced countries. Hence there is a certain ambivalence towards the metropolitan countries: political opposition, but a recognition of their economic superiority. Ruling Leninist parties then copy the advanced industrial methods of the capitalist countries, while at the same time avoiding capitalist *relations* (in the sense of ownership) to the means of production. Mao's supporters go further than Lenin in this respect and argue that forms of division of labour, of participation in administration, of relations between men may be 'socialist' before the technological basis of socialism has outstripped that of capitalism.

These last two points bring out another theme which has run through this chapter: the relevance of Lenin's ideas about revolution to the course of events in Russia after 1917 and the rise of the phenomenon known as Stalinism. Lenin's assumptions, his world view, were essentially the same as Stalin's; but, when in power, the events, people, happenings and constellation of forces were different. In the next chapters we shall turn to consider how this pattern of beliefs was translated into action, or frustrated by conditions, when Lenin and the Bolsheviks took power.

The above classification is one way of ordering Lenin's theory and practice in relation to the advancement of the proletarian revolution of the early twentieth century. How can we order analytically Lenin's work as a sociologist, how is Lenin different in method, outlook and conclusion from other sociologists?

First, Lenin combined Marx's and Durkheim's attack on the liberal-democratic version of society. Like Marx, Lenin emphasised the class struggle. Like Durkheim, he assumed that the whole takes precedence over the parts. He was an opponent of liberalism and individualism: as Nisbet has put it, Durkheim's 'sociology constitutes a massive attack upon the philosophical foundations of liberalism' (Nisbet 1965: 28). Lenin emphasised not only the importance of thought but also of discipline, of order, of obedience. He was strongly opposed to anarchistic interpretations of social relations and was as hostile to the anarchists and populists as he was to the landed classes and the capitalists. While Durkheim eulogised 'society' and sought to uncover those pathologies pulling it apart, Lenin had as a frame of reference the progression of societies through history and sought to define the role of the working class and its political instrument, the Party. Lenin saw man in a dialectical relationship with nature: he played an active role in making history, but he was at the same time conditioned by the laws of nature, which are external to him.

Secondly, Lenin's method combined critical analysis of society – derived from Marx – with advances in bourgeois science. He attempted to come to terms with 'laws of nature' as stipulated by natural scientists, to embody them within the framework of dialectical materialism. He extended this anlysis to include various methods of what we now call the social sciences. He applied Marxist analysis to the concrete examination of societies; he synthesised philosophy, methods and the collection of empirical data and made historical materialism the study of the dynamics of capitalist society as he knew it. He was a firm believer in the collection and use of statistics, and he advocated the utilisation of organisation theory and scientific management. Lenin unites the class analysis of Marx with a Weberian-style theory of organisation, of management. He advocated the benefits of specialisation, professionalism and administration under socialism. But he underestimated, unlike Weber, the ways that these phenomena might become subjects (rather than objects) of power. Lenin's theory of organisation is incomplete. He ignores the vested interests of those in bureaucratic positions. Lenin tended to see bureaucracy as a dysfunction in the popular sense caused by the wrong people being in command, or by pig-headedness, lack of education and other such traits inherited from the Tsarist order. Marxists generally emphasise the role of the producer to the neglect of the needs of citizens. Marxists have perhaps over-emphasised the rights of producers and should build into their conceptual armoury the needs of citizens as consumers. Lenin's views on participation need to be elaborated to include all kinds of groups under modern capitalism (and socialism) who are subject to administrative power. The government apparatus is not something which can operate like the postal service, but it includes administrative coercion and the power of 'professionals' which can define the needs and wants of citizens, rather than fulfilling their needs. The control of administration must be seen as a major priority of advocates of socialism: bodies modelled on the Soviets which originated as strike committees in Tsarist Russia are part of the rhetoric of revolution, and are not appropriate bodies, in my view, for the complex task of articulating citizens' needs and controlling the administration of a modern advanced society.

Thirdly, Lenin combines a Marxist class analysis with Rousseau's notion of the general will. It is a fair comment on Rousseau that he knew that a general will existed but he was unable to elucidate who knew what it was. For Lenin, the general will could only be the will of the working class and this was to be articulated through the Party. Similarly, in his concept of the role of the state, he thought that under the proletariat, it would play an active role in educating and creating the consciousness of the citizen – it was not simply the expression of the 'will of all'.

Fourthly, like Durkheim, Lenin saw that social collapse was likely to occur during a movement from one type of society to another. For Durkheim this was at the junction of a society organised on the principles of 'mechanical solidarity' and one based on 'organic solidarity'. Lenin saw this not as a breakdown or as a pathological state, but welcomed it as a condition of socialist revolution. Unlike Marx and Engels, who considered a socialist revolution in the context of the advanced industrial nations like England, Lenin's approach shared more with Durkheim in that he saw breakdown and revolution occurring when pre-capitalist and capitalist societies were juxtaposed. But, unlike Durkheim, Lenin emphasised the capitalist process on a world scale. In considering the impact of the advanced countries on others he turned the centre of gravity in Marxist thought from Europe to the colonial and oppressed peoples; and unlike the introspective, impotent and pessimistic development of most Marxist thought in Western Europe it opened up a new perspective on socialism and revolutionary change in the Third World.

Fifthly, Lenin adopted in his analysis of society a revolutionary praxis (i.e. instrumental or applicable knowledge: the unity of Marxist theory and revolutionary action). This might be contrasted with the conservative 'practice' of contemporary sociological analysis which is implicitly derived from Weber's ideas of ethical neutrality. Weber and contemporary sociology are concerned with the analysis and classification of social phenomena, seeking to be neutral in the application of knowledge, and leaving political decisions to politicians. Moreover, Western Marxist thinking since Lenin's death has been preoccupied with interpretation of literature, of culture, of the 'alienation' and domination of man under capitalism. This is foreign to Lenin's thought: rather than the 'alienation' of man, he stressed latent and manifest class consciousness. Lenin's practice is revolutionary: the ends and means of social science should be to advance the historic mission of the working class – as he put it, 'without a revolutionary theory, there can be no revolutionary movement'. But Lenin also grasped the fact that the modern capitalist state is based on coercion; thus the humanistic appeal to reason, to debate and to discussion, though valuable, is essentially limited: for a socialist revolution to be successful (and here he had Russia particularly in mind) armed force had to be utilised. To maintain power the proletariat had to create its own state power, it had to institute the 'dictatorship of the proletariat', the concept of which is an essential pillar in Lenin's world view. Under this dictatorship, Lenin recognised that the state might have to use terror. The recognition of the need to use force is perhaps the greatest difference between Lenin's thought and that of those brought up in the

Weberian tradition; and the demand for political commitment and action is probably why his thought is uncongenial in tone, outlook, method and practice to many Western Marxists and non-Marxists alike – not only to defenders of capitalism but also to its radical liberal and social-democratic critics.

Lenin's methods of analysis have to be seen in the context of human *action*. Lenin was concerned with furthering social change. Unlike structuralists of various kinds, Lenin did not regard the processes of the natural and social world to be determined by universal laws independent of human action. Rather, such laws conditioned human action and awareness of them was essential for such action to be fruitful. Lenin's theory of action also related individual action at the micro level to macro social change. The 'action frame of reference' of modern sociologists has no action in it in a Leninist sense: it is an 'orientation' of an actor (an individual or a collectivity) which is 'motivated' and directed by subjective interpretations of the meanings of the external world.* Weberian social action tends to be limited to individual action at a micro level and Weber and Parsons do not successfully provide a universal link between individual constellations of 'actions' and macro social change.† Whereas for Lenin, actors are conditioned by the laws of motion of society which both restrict their activity and also provide opportunities for action. The nexus between individual action at the micro level and macro social change was provided by the Party which aggregated individual perceptions (and given individual needs) into a programme of policy and political work to carry it out.

---

* Weber defines action as 'social in so far as, by virtue of the subjective meaning attached to it by the acting individual (or individuals), it takes account of the behaviour of others, and is thereby oriented in its course' (Weber 1947: 88; see also Parsons 1951: Chapter 1).
† The rise of capitalism, for instance, is an ex-post explanation of a particular occurrence, rather than a generalised theory of social change. It has no implications for action now.

3

vvvvvvvvvvvvvvvvvvvvvvvvvvvvvvvvvvvvvvvvvvvvvvvvvvvvvvvvvvvvvvvvvvvvvvvvvvvvvv

Stalin's Bolshevism: legitimation and critique

THE SOVIET BOLSHEVIK POSITION: SOCIALIST CONSTRUCTION

The successful seizure of power by the Bolsheviks posed quite different problems for their leadership from the ones that they had grappled with before 1917. Now Lenin was confronted by the tasks of maintaining power against adversaries, of governing a large population, and of entering into political relations with foreign states. It is impossible to describe the different phases of Soviet history under Lenin (War Communism and the New Economic Policy). I would like to highlight what has become a major feature of socialist states: the application of a version of Marxism as a praxis of development.

We have seen that for Lenin the economic level of the productive forces was an essential 'conditioning' component of the superstructure. As capitalist industrialisation had been able to develop under the autocracy without a strong indigenous capitalist class, Lenin and his supporters were quite consistent in saying that industrialisation could proceed as well without it under the Bolshevik Party. In 1923, Lenin regarded the view that the USSR did not possess the objective economic conditions for socialism as pedantic, and he dubbed as 'timorous reformists' those social democrats who put forward such views (*Our Revolution*, CW33: 476).

In the context of Soviet Russia and of other countries developing today, 'socialism' has come to have a quite different meaning from that which it has in the advanced industrial countries of Western Europe. In the former, 'socialism' means political power wielded by the Party for previously underprivileged strata (often manual and non-manual workers and peasants), utilised for industrial and social development,

70

and industrialisation is a crucial component in socialist construction. As Kelle *et al.* (1970: 256) put it: 'Socialism . . . presupposes a conscious and comprehensive management of social development'. Socialism is a moment in history, it is a process of development following the seizure of power by the Communist Party. Lenin describes the early phases of socialism as 'merely state-capitalist monopoly *which is made to serve the interests of the whole people* and has to that extent *ceased* to be capitalist monopoly' (*The Impending Catastrophe, SW2:* 211). Here Lenin envisaged socialism growing out of the highest stage of monopoly capitalism, characterised by the amalgamation of all banks under government ownership or control, the nationalisation of the large firms, the formation of compulsory associations of industrialists and traders and compulsory unions of consumers. In *Better Fewer, but Better*, written just before Lenin died, he recognises the brake of *cultural* backwardness on Russia: 'We lack enough civilization to pass straight on to socialism, although we have the political requisites for it' (*SW3:* 731). Lenin recognises a higher level of development of social relations, in a general sense, which would come with socialism. But Lenin legitimises the *political* structure of Russia to achieve it: by omitting the second part of this quotation, Lewin (1973: 108) wrongly implies that Lenin believed that socialism could not be built in Russia and that the main task was to hold out 'until reinforcements arrived'. Lenin saw Soviet power as a first step, a stage preceding communism: 'the only scientific distinction between socialism and communism is that the first term implies the first stage of the new society arising out of capitalism, while the second implies the next and higher stage' (*A Great Beginning, SW3:* 174). 'We in Russia . . . are making the first steps in the transition from capitalism to socialism or the lower stage of communism' (*'Left-Wing' Communism, SW3:* 314). Even in 1917, Lenin considered that a new type of state of the masses 'had already been established' (*The Tasks of the Proletariat, SW2:* 60).

Social-democratic theorists, on the other hand, conceive of 'socialism' as sets of reciprocated relations between individuals in a society, characterised by equality, participation and a collective orientation. (See discussion in Kolakowski and Hampshire 1974 and Tellenback 1978.) As Lukes has put it: 'The ideal of equality has always been central to the socialist tradition: thus Professor Taylor specifies "greater equality in the conditions of life" as the first goal of "any socialist in a Western country today"' (Lukes 1974b: 74). Much of Western Marxist criticism of state socialism, particularly in Anglo-Saxon countries, is in effect in this vein: it is concerned with socialism as a 'way of life' and is derived from the political culture of liberalism and Christian ethics. Lenin is clear that discussion of the 'transition from capitalism to socialism on the basis of general talk about liberty, equality, democracy in general, equality of labour democracy ... [reveals a] petty-bourgeois, philistine nature and [such people] ideologically and slavishly follow in the wake of the bourgeoisie' (*A Great Beginning, SW3*: 175).

A 'developmental approach' stems from Lenin's interpretation of Marxism in which the level of material forces has primacy: policy under socialism was geared to the development of the economic base. It cannot be emphasised too strongly that, in Lenin's thought, the evils ensuing from large-scale industrial production (the enslavement of labour by the machine, the oppression of the working class, the prostitution of marriage, the ruination of the handicraftsman, and the degradation of the small-scale peasant) were attributed to capitalism, whereas under socialism, the benefits of large-scale industrial production would accrue to the people as a whole and would be used to further social development. In this way one of the most important roles of Lenin as a Marxist theorist and of Leninism as an ideology was to rationalise and to legitimate the power of the Bolshevik Party to create an industrial society.

This was stated clearly by Lenin in 1920, when he defined communism as 'Soviet power plus the electrification of all the country' (*Our Foreign and Domestic Position and the Tasks of the Party, CW31*: 419, see also *The Eighth All-Russian Congress of Soviets, CW31*: 516). In this slogan, Lenin sums up the political and the industrial components of his policy. The emphasis in Western studies of the Soviet Union is often on the political side of the equation, stressing the link between communism and 'Soviet power'; but the economic goals are also important and especially so for what was an underdeveloped country. Without a priority being given to heavy industry, illustrated in the above slogan by the widespread distribution of electrical power, 'socialist construction would remain only a sum of decrees' (*Our Foreign and Domestic Position, CW31*: 419–20). The supply of electricity to the countryside would also have the effect of enhancing levels of production in agriculture and would provide a technical basis for its industrialisation.

Lenin also recognised that industrialisation could not be achieved without an ethic of work. In 1918, in *The Immediate Tasks of Soviet Power*, he acknowledged that 'the Russian is a bad worker compared to the workers of the advanced nations'. Therefore, a major task of the government was 'to teach the people how to work' (*CW*27: 259). Love for one's work is one of the highest principles of Leninist morality, given its best-known form in the slogan 'he who does not work, neither shall he eat'. This may be contrasted with Western social-democratic thought and much of liberal social philosophy, where the emphasis is on the legitimacy of levels and rates of rewards from work: it is taken for granted that all should work and socialist policy is geared towards redistributing the rewards of work equally. Lenin also linked this ethic to the organisation of work. The abolition of classes, he argued, would 'for the first time open up the way for competition on a really mass scale' (*CW* 27: 259). To reach this goal, the most advanced managerial techniques of capitalism had to be adopted. Even the practices of Taylorism, which Lenin described as 'the last word in capitalism', had to be utilised. For 'its greatest scientific achievements [lie] in the field of analysing mechanical motions during work, in the elimination of superfluous and awkward motions, in the working out of correct methods of work, and in the introduction of the best system of accounting and control etc.' (*CW* 27: 259). Lenin called for combining Soviet rule with the 'latest progressive measures of capitalism' and the Soviet government, he said, 'must introduce in Russia the study and teaching of the Taylor system and its systematic trial and adoption'. Here again we may contrast Lenin's approach to work with that of critics of the work process under capitalism. Here objection is focussed on the organisation of work with the intention of making the job more interesting: alienation of labour is seen in the process of production. Lenin, however, adopted a macro-analysis: motivation and exploitation were determined by the system of property and economy – through commodity exchange – rather than by the type of job done and the technical organisation of labour.

Lenin stressed the importance of work and absolutely condemned idleness. He put in one category 'the rich, the swindlers, the idlers and the rowdies' whom he dubbed as the 'dregs of humanity . . . [like] an ulcer inherited from capitalism' (*How to Organise Competition, SW*2: 471), and he strongly condemned 'Slovenliness, carelessness, untidiness, unpunctuality, nervous haste, the inclination to substitute discussion for action and talk for work'. The Bolshevik leadership also deplored immediate and unrestrained sexual fulfilment, which is another aspect of the desired psychological predisposition of deferred gratification necessary for development. As a writer in *Izvestiya* put it in 1925, 'Drown your sexual energy in public work. . . . If you want to solve your sexual problem, be a public worker, be a comrade, not a stallion or a brood mare' (cited in Carr 1958: 34). These quotations are sufficient to make the point that the nature of the industrial order which the Bolsheviks under Lenin wanted to build had many of the features of advanced capitalism existing in the West; the ideology is quite hostile to anarchist and populist thought, which has developed as a protest against industrialisation as much as against capitalism. Its emphasis in favour of industrial development also sets it aside from social democracy of the British Labour Party type which, in theory, emphasises more humane concerns and social equality.

There is clear emphasis in Lenin's Marxism of the 'primacy of production forces'; under socialism, the class struggle is replaced by state development of the forces of production. It is assumed that the *technique* developed under capitalism may be applied quite independently of capitalist relations of production.

Other leading Soviet Bolsheviks also shared Lenin's views on the form the construction of socialism would take. As Knei-Paz has pointed out, Trotsky after 1917 resigned himself 'to the fact that the party (or government) must continue substituting itself in the economic and social revolution' (1978: 261). Trotsky used compulsion: he had suppressed the Kronstadt uprising; he had advocated the militarisation of unions and that workers should be compelled to work. The period of the transition to socialism was 'characterised by the use of unpalatable but necessary and desirable methods' (*ibid.*: 268). He supported a policy of the government carrying out 'primitive socialist accumulation'. Like Lenin, he advocated the assimilation of Western scientific techniques. 'The Soviet system shod with American technique will be socialism' (*Culture and Socialism*, cited by Knei-Paz: 289). The form of state power, Party hegemony, the economic and social revolution from above were legitimated by Trotsky. While his critique of Stalin was penetrating (see below pp. 86–88) Trotsky's own position, when in power, shared many assumptions common to Lenin and Stalin.

The advent of Stalin certainly signalled a new turn in Bolshevik policy, but this cannot be understood independently of Lenin's theory and practice. To argue otherwise would be analogous to saying that Anglicanism may be understood without any knowledge of Christ's teaching. Though wrong in other respects, Gouldner has rightly drawn attention to the fact that the decisions and policy of the Bolsheviks cannot be comprehended 'apart from an understanding of their special reading of Marxism, i.e. "scientific socialism"' (1978: 46).

The Soviet Bolshevik position: socialist construction

Stalin was not just a political activist maximising his own power for his personal use – whether rationally or irrationally conceived. A great deal of his own writing is taken up with the exposition and development of Lenin's thinking. His writings include a treatise on *Dialectical and Historical Materialism* (1938), *The Foundations of Leninism* (1924), *Problems of Leninism* (1924), *Marxism and the National Question* (1913), *Marxism and Linguistics* (1950), *Economic Problems of Socialism in the USSR* (1952). In his methodology, summed up in *Dialectical and Historical Materialism*, Stalin shows his affinity, like Lenin, with Engels's materialism. And again, like Lenin, he emphasises the importance of the mode of production: 'The history of the development of society is above all the history of the development of production. . . . The clue to the study of the laws of history of society must not be sought in men's minds, in the views and ideas of society, but in the mode of production practised by society in any given historical period: it must be sought in the economic life of society' (reprinted in Franklin 1973: 320).

Stalin's ideas of social laws are similar to Lenin's. Laws are independent of man. 'Marxism regards laws of science – whether they be laws of natural science or laws of political economy – as the reflection of objective processes which take place independently of the will of man. Man may discover laws, get to know them, study them, reckon with them in his activities and utilize them in the interests of society, but he cannot change or abolish them. Still less can he form or create new laws of science' (*Economic Problems*, reprinted in Franklin: 446). Stalin, like Engels, regards laws in political economy as having constraining effects on man; society at best can harness laws of nature, use them to its benefit, but it cannot change them (*ibid.*: 448).

Lenin devised the form of Communist Party as a weapon of struggle in Tsarist Russia. Stalin enshrined his version of it under conditions of what he called 'achieving the dictatorship of the proletariat' (*Foundations of Leninism*, 1934: 171). Stalin saw the Party as the 'political leader' of the working class, as the 'General Staff' of the proletariat, as 'an inseparable part' of 'the working class' (*ibid.*: 172–3). The Party for Lenin was the leader of the working class in the revolution, for Stalin the Party became the '*instrument of the dictatorship of the proletariat*'. Stalin emphasises discipline in the Party after the dictatorship of the proletariat has been achieved. He cites Lenin approvingly as follows: 'Whoever weakens in the least the iron discipline of the Party of the proletariat (especially during the time of its dictatorship) actually aids the bourgeoisie against the proletariat' (*ibid.*: 181). The Party emphasised the unity of the will of the proletariat, and all factions and 'divisions of authority' were precluded.

Stalin's ideology and world view had an affinity with Lenin's in method and orientation. Both men shared a similar approach to Marxism: they accepted Engels's interpretation of historical and dialectical materialism; they emphasised the constraining effects of laws external to man; politically they shared similar views – they saw Soviet Russia as threatened by an international world order of capitalism; and they recognised the necessity for the dictatorship of the proletariat and a strong state; economically, they both stressed the importance of developing the level of productive forces and the need to borrow and copy the advanced techniques of the West.

But in many ways also, the 'routinisation' of Lenin's ideas into the legitimating ideology of Leninism resulted in a departure from Lenin's values and outlook. The theory of imperialism helped to justify the building of socialism in one country, but the form the Soviet industrial and political system took under Stalin departed considerably from Lenin's original views. While Lenin emphasised that one country should begin to build socialism, and he heartily supported attempts to create the conditions for building socialism in backward countries (*Our Revolution*, CW33: 477), he did not envisage, as does the doctrine of Leninism under Stalin, that socialism in its widest sense could be *completed* in one country and be equated with ownership relations. And here, of course, Stalin was completely at odds with Trotsky and his followers. While the component of imperialism has undoubtedly acted as a rallying cry for colonialist and ex-colonialist countries, Lenin did not envisage a situation in which the Soviet form of the dictatorship of the proletariat would be regarded as the 'international doctrine of the proletarians of all lands [which] is suitable and obligatory for all countries without exception, including those where capitalism is developed' (Stalin 1934b: 104). While Lenin identified an important cleavage between developed and under-developed countries, he also pointed to the world proletariat as the prime revolutionary force, as epitomised in the slogan: 'Workers of the world unite!' In both Stalin's *Foundations of Leninism* and *Problems of Leninism*, very little attention is given to this task and the emphasis is shifted to the importance of completing the construction of socialism in one country. With the passage of time, emphasis has moved from the world proletariat to the national liberation movements. Stalin looked to other revolutions breaking out in countries undergoing early capitalism, rather than in the advanced capitalist states. These changes in emphasis are clearly linked to the international status and policy interest of the Soviet government.

Stalin, however, cannot be regarded as departing completely from Lenin's own outlook. Lenin himself emphasised the shift of revolutionary focus to the East. Quoting Kautsky with approval, he said 'The centre of revolutionary thought and action is shifting more and more to the Slavs ... Russia, which has borrowed so much revolutionary initiative from the West, is now perhaps herself ready to serve the West as a source of revolutionary energy' (*'Left-Wing' Communism*, SW31: 22). (Trotsky, after 1924, also took a similar 'Eastward' perspective.) Lenin also saw Russia as a paradigm of revolution which could be copied elsewhere: 'all the primary features of our revolution and many of its secondary features, are of international significance in the meaning of its effect on all countries' (*ibid.*, SW31: 21). (On the international dimensions of the Russian Revolution, see Harding 1980: Chapter 11.)

Under Stalin, democratic centralism was transformed from a mechanism to ensure rationality (in the sense of the expression of class consciousness) to the mobilisation of people into an industrial society. Voting at elections, for instance, instead of being a method of popular recall and control becomes both a kind of audience participation and an expression of loyalty to the Soviet order. As Stalin put it in 1939, elections to the supreme organs 'were a magnificent demonstration of that unity of Soviet society and of that amity among the nations of the USSR which constitute the characteristic feature of the internal situation of our country' (*Report to the Eighteenth Congress*, 10 March 1939, reprinted in Franklin 1973: 368). Participation in the economic planning procedure through various forms of meeting and discussion, although often ritualistic, is important from a mobilising and symbolic point of view. Such activities communicate and identify the masses with specific goals. They are not, however, 'socialist' in the *ideal* way desired by Lenin, and the USSR has failed to produce any really advanced form of direct administration by the masses.* The proletarian state for Lenin was an apparatus necessary in the early stages of the dictatorship of the proletariat: but as society advanced to communism it would wither away. For Stalin, the state continued *in theory* even under communism. Stalin is well known for his statement that the class struggle sharpens as socialism develops, and therefore concluded that, under these con-

---

* That is in the sense of determining political 'inputs' to the political process; the Soviet Union has been more successful in mobilising people in the 'output' of the administration. See Friedgut (1979).

ditions, the state could remain also in the period of communism (*Report to Eighteenth Congress*, 10 March 1939, reprinted in Franklin 1973: 386–7). While Stalin attributed legitimacy to the Party, in fact the Party during his rule played no significant role as a collective articulator of policy.

Leninism, as developed in the Soviet Union after Lenin's death, has been an ideology in which the construction of socialism is almost synonymous with industrialisation. Soviet Marxism–Leninism, therefore, provides an ideology that justifies industrialisation on a large scale. Centralisation, nationalisation, hegemonic state control, the shaping of social homogeneity and an adamant belief in the virtues of modern technology are fundamental characteristics of the model that has been devised. All these factors play an important part in Lenin's theory and practice. Lenin, Trotsky and Stalin all used as a point of reference the organisational model of what they believed was the most advanced form of capitalism in the West; and the value pattern of what Stalin called 'Russian revolutionary sweep' plus 'American efficiency' (*Foundations of Leninism*: 184) is akin to the 'instrumental activism' of advanced capitalist countries. Hence it is not surprising that, as the Soviet Union has matured as an industrial state, it has appeared to 'converge' in many respects with industrial practices under capitalism. Lenin, however, also advocated direct forms of political participation and greater equality. These were dropped under Stalin: the notion of a utopian form of communism is absent from Stalin's writings.

My argument has been to attempt to show a continuity in some respects in policy running from Lenin through Trotsky to Stalin. This continuity is essentially the adaptation of Marxism to be an ideology legitimating the construction of a type of industrial and 'modern' society, involving the copying of capitalist techniques and a complex division of labour. Many Marxist and non-Marxist critiques have arisen in reaction to the apparent similarities between Stalin's Russia and Western capitalism and against the means used by Stalin.

Marxists and neo-Marxists have attempted to explain and account for the impact of revolution in many ways, and in doing so have selected many 'facts' of Soviet history to illustrate their viewpoint. First, there are those whom we may term the Marxist–Leninist school. They see Stalin as a continuation of Lenin's praxis, they vindicate Lenin's position, his interpretation of Marx, but see many negative aspects of Stalinism which are derived from Stalin's *personality*: examples are Krushchev and Roy Medvedev. Second, are the theorists of the 'transitional society', who again support Lenin's line but see policy under Stalin as departing from it: here we shall consider the views of Mandel, Lock and Bettelheim. Both of these schools of thought consider the Revolution essentially as a phenomenon which had many positive social, economic and political effects, while others were undesirable and unintended by the leaders (particularly Lenin) of the Revolution.

Turning to non-Marxist writers who come to similar conclusions about the continuity between Lenin and Stalin, there are the explicitly anti-Soviet writers subscribing to 'totalitarianism': the best-known example is Solzhenitsyn (*The Gulag Archipelago*). In addition, there is what might be called the 'social history' school, which adopts a multi-causal explanation and adds a cultural dimension to the evolution of Russia: examples here are writers such as E. H. Carr, Roger Pethy-bridge, and R. C. Tucker. Some of these put forward a 'weak' typology of totalitarianism, combining negative features and positive achievements. It is impossible to deal in detail with all these views, but the major features will be brought out, and then I shall turn to attempt a synthesis of the approaches.

CRITICISMS BY SOVIET BOLSHEVIKS

Many Marxists supporting Bolshevism delineate between Lenin's intentions and Stalin's policies, many of the latter being forms of dege-neration. The mildest criticism is that of Khrushchev and Medvedev. For these writers, Lenin represented all that was good in Bolshevism, Stalin all that was bad. Lenin's own writings done in the last days of his life are used to buttress this argument. (See Kelle *et al.*: 260–2. Lewin (1973) has developed the significance of Lenin's last writings.)

Khrushchev's revelations to the Twentieth Congress of the CPSU were the first offical confirmation of the 'excesses' perpetrated by Stalin and Beria. Khrushchev, however critical of Stalin, does not disagree with the major policies carried out under him. His fight against 'Trotsky-ites, Zinovievites and rightists and the bourgeois nationalists . . . was indispensable' (Krushchev 1977: 637). Khrushchev opposed the 'practi-cal consequences resulting from the cult of the individual' (*ibid.*: 580). These included the wrongful imprisonment, deportation and death of many innocent people through 'mass repression' (p. 587). Through these excesses the Party lost many valuable workers and the prep-aration of the country's defences was jeopardised (p. 606), serious mistakes were made during the Great Patriotic War and violations of nationality policy were made through mass deportations of nations (p. 619).

At root, Stalin's aberrant policies stemmed from his personality and no structural or institutional reasons are given at all. Khrushchev cites Lenin's criticisms of December 1922: 'Stalin is excessively rude and this defect, which can be freely tolerated in our minds and in contacts among us Communists, becomes a defect which cannot be tolerated in one holding the position of the General Secretary' (Khrushchev 1977: 583). These 'negative characteristics' which were incipient in Lenin's lifetime, 'transformed themselves during the last years into a grave abuse of power by Stalin, which caused untold harm to our Party' (p. 585). The lack of collegiality and the brutal violence practised by Stalin was the result of his 'capricious and despotic character' (*ibid.*). He had a 'mania for greatness.... He had completely lost consciousness of reality' (p.624). Khrushchev concedes that 'power accumulated in the hands of one person' (p.609), 'the leadership practice which came into being during the last years of Stalin's life became a serious obstacle in the path of Soviet social development' (p.637). But Khrushchev does not say how Stalin was able to maintain his position. In the early years, he says, 'Stalin was one of the strongest Marxists and his logic, his strength and his will greatly influenced the cadres and Party work' (p.637). Khrushchev continues: 'Later, however, Stalin, abusing his power more and more, began to fight eminent Party and government leaders and to use terroristic methods against honest Soviet people' (p.637). Stalin misused his personal power, the Politbureau met 'only occasionally', and 'in the last years the Central Committee plenary sessions were not convened'. It was difficult for 'any member of the Politbureau to take a stand against one or another unjust or improper procedure, against serious errors and shortcomings in the practices of leadership' (p.638). Khrushchev's analysis may be summed up as: Stalin's major policies were a proper continuation of Marxism–Leninism, but he made serious errors, many of which were criminal, and these were the products of his personality. Stalinism was an aberration, but once Stalin himself was eliminated the cause of the phenomenon would also be removed. This is a somewhat similar position to that of Lenin, who was aware that the General Secretary had great prerogatives of power, but he only suggested changing the holder of the post, rather than the structure of power going with it. (See discussion in Lewin, 1973: 127.)

Roy Medvedev adopts a similar viewpoint, but his explanation is much more complex and many other conditioning factors are introduced into his extended analysis (Medvedev 1971). Bracketing Medvedev with Khrushchev is to some extent unfair to the former's analysis, but it does emphasise Medvedev's commitment to the core of the Soviet system, as achieved by and as intended by Lenin. Stalin was, for Medvedev, a vicious criminal and a deviation from the norms of socialist morality as defined by Lenin. 'Stalin's long rule led to the most serious distortions in the theory and practice of socialist construction. Many of the basic principles of a socialist society were perverted, and enormous harm was done to the cause of socialism' (1971: 436). On this view, Stalin willed Stalinism: rather than being 'situation–determined' it was 'personally–determined'. Stalin 'created and encouraged the system of arbitrary rule and terror that caused the death of millions. . . . [He] was totally pre-occupied with the preservation of his unlimited power, and contemptuous of almost everyone around him and of human life in general. . . . Torture was introduced in the NKVD [security organs] on Stalin's insistence. . . . [His] orders and actions were deliberate crimes. . . . We must take into account not only the ambition but also the cruelty and viciousness of Stalin' (Medvedev 1971: 297, 301, 303, 304, 326).

Medvedev, however, recognises a kind of duality in the revolutionary process in Russia. The socialist system, he argued, had a momentum that Stalin could not stop and this led to 'the rapid development of Soviet society in some areas'. Medvedev mentions the new factories, schools, the new army, developments in science and the arts; and the position of the oppressed nationalities was also improved (Medvedev 1971: 371–2).

These aspects do not figure very prominently in his work, which is mainly concerned with the explanation and effects of Stalin's misrule. Medvedev's explanation is eclectic. It is a combination of 'historical accidents', though he recognises important historical conditions. 'It was an historical accident that Stalin, the embodiment of all the worst elements in the Russian revolutionary movement, came to power after Lenin, the embodiment of all that was best' (p.362). The motivation for Stalin's crimes was his 'measureless ambition', his 'hidden lust for unlimited power' (p.324). Stalin gained control through 'intrigues and crimes' (p.333). In *On Stalin and Stalinism,* Medvedev writes: 'In most respects, however, there is no continuity between Leninism and Stalinism; they are essentially different political phenomena sharing a common "Marxist" terminology. Stalin's policies were in no way a reflection of Leninist objectives' (1979: 188).

Medvedev concedes that Stalin had a mass support and that certain historical conditions were favourable to the rise of Stalin, but he does not, in my view, bring out their importance and neither does he construct a theory which gives them an unambiguous place. He recognises, for instance, the 'petty-bourgeois' character of Tsarist Russia, the low educational and cultural level of the masses, the absence of a strong democratic tradition, the centuries-old cult of the Tsar and the ideology of absolutism (p.364). Stalin did not carry out his crimes alone: people glorified him. 'Millions of ordinary people took part in meetings and demonstrations demanding severe reprisals against "enemies". . . . The majority of Soviet people believed in Stalin and the NKVD in those years, and were sincere in the indignation against "enemies of the people"' (p.365). The masses were Stalin's 'ultimate determinant of his success' (p.375).

None of these tendencies finds a place in a coherent theory of revolution or social change. Medvedev is very much a voluntarist. Oddly, he does attribute many of the more positive features of Soviet power to the influence of 'the ideology and the collective will of the Party, Lenin's heritage, the socialist aspirations of the workers' (p. 371). Medvedev seeks to locate the degeneration of the Soviet Union in a moral criticism of Stalin. Stalin, he says, was not a Marxist: he lacked commitment to a Marxist system of 'convictions and moral principles' (p. 333). Medvedev's paramount task is to nail Stalin with moral crimes – against humanity and against socialism – hence the role of denunciation takes precedence over explanation. Two major criticisms then may be made of Medvedev's book: first, it seems inconceivable that the 'positive achievements' should not be linked to the activities of the Soviet government headed by Stalin. Secondly, there is a complete lack of any analysis of the ideology and the theories developed by Stalin. It is a shallow political theory which explains dictatorships on the motivation for a personal lust for power and it is also a non-Marxist one.

THEORIES OF THE TRANSITIONAL SOCIETY

Other Marxists have eschewed the criticism of the Stalin era in voluntarist, humanistic terms of the cult of the personality, and have sought more structural explanations of the phenomenon. These range from a positive to a negative appraisal of Stalin, but may all be subsumed under the paradigm of a transitional society. This characterisation is shared by Althusser (1975), Bettelheim (1972, 1975), Trotsky (1968) and Mandel (1968, 1974, 1978), and an attempt here will be made to analyse their not always unanimous* views of the transitional society. This is not a new term, as it was used by Lenin to describe the first stage of the formation of communist society (Lenin, *The Role and Functions of Trade Unions under NEP, CW33*: 184–5). In 1919, he pointed out that 'theoretically there can be no doubt that between capitalism and communism there lies a definite transition period which must combine the features and properties of both these forms of social economy. This transition period has to be a period of struggle between dying capitalism and nascent communism – or, in other words, between capitalism which has been defeated but not destroyed and communism which has been born but is still very feeble' (*Economics and Politics in the Era of the Dictatorship of the Proletariat, CW30*: 107, see also below pp. 85–6).

But this early conception of transitional society is distinct from the use of the term by contemporary theorists. They bring out the fact that Marx and Engels did not contemplate that a society organised along the lines of the present-day USSR could be socialist. Bettelheim has made this quite clear. 'This complex reality, this combination of socialist state property and social planning, on the one hand, with commodity categories (or at least the appearance of them), on the other, may seem to contradict some of the descriptions of socialist society given in advance by Marx or Engels' (1975: 32). Marx and Engels thought that in socialist society, even as it began to emerge from capitalism, there would be 'neither commodities, nor value, nor money, nor consequently, prices and wages'. Thus, argues Bettelheim, 'There is . . . seemingly, a contradiction between the actual working of the socialist economies which we know today and the analyses made by Marx and Engels' (*ibid.*: 33).

This difference between the 'transitional society' of Bettelheim and Mandel and that of Marx has been elaborated in the criticism of Buick (1975), who points out that the 'transition period' is 'the period *after* the capture of political power by the working class and *before* the actual establishment of the common ownership of the means of production' (1975: 60). But in the first stage of socialist society (according to Marx) not only are there no commodities or money, but also there is no state and society is classless (*ibid.*: 61). A socialist society on this basis, argues Buick, cannot exist if there is 'commodity production', and if goods are produced for a market (see *ibid.*: 65–6). Hence the defined conditions of

*It is particularly important to note that Bettelheim and Mandel disagree on the *present* class character of the USSR: the former, after Mao, defines it as 'state capitalist' and the latter, following Trotsky, as a 'degenerate workers' state'.

Bettelheim's transitional society, from this viewpoint, make it non-socialist.

This difference in the nature of the transitional society – between what Marx anticipated and the actual structure of the USSR – would be conceded by both Bettelheim and Mandel. Bettelheim makes similar points to Buick and agrees that in the economy of the transition both Marx and Engels thought that there would be no commodity production (1975: 32–3). Lock argues that there is no such thing as a 'socialist mode of production' and he regards the transition period as a 'contradictory combination of two modes of production, the capitalist and communist' (*ibid*: 17). Similarly, Bettelheim considers the evolution of socialism to be an infinitely longer process than that originally envisaged by Marx and Engels and he argues that modes of production overlap. Even in advanced capitalist countries such as Britain, 'There is ... a "gap" between the capitalist mode of production in the reality of its concept and the actual economic system' (*ibid*: 15). In any given social system there may be several modes of production but only one is dominant. The dominant mode 'permeates the entire system and modifies the conditions in which the subordinate modes of production function and develop' (*ibid*.: 16). Here Bettelheim seems to be hinting at the fact that certain areas of social life have forms of autonomy related to 'outdated' modes of production. Mandel points out that a society in transition between capitalism and socialism is characterised by the 'relative *immaturity* of its production relations' (1974: 7).

These writers, however, refer to 'distortions': Mandel mentions the 'severe or extreme forms of bureaucratic deformation and degeneration' (1974: 8), and Bettelheim considers the '*lack of conformity* between the essentials of the new social relations which are henceforth dominant and the productive forces' (1975: 23). Althusser in refuting the Soviet 'pseudo-concept' of the cult of personality points out that it exposed 'certain practices', 'abuses', 'errors' and 'crimes', but explained 'nothing of their conditions, of their causes, in short of their *internal* determination, and therefore their forms' (1975: 80). All these writers point out that the dynamic and the dialectic of change is to be found in the resolution of class conflict, and between class forces. This has been put clearly by Mandel when he points out that class forces are governed by 'two antagonistic economic logics: the logic of the plan and the logic of the market. ... The two sets of laws evidently correspond to two class interests. ... The first, the interest of the proletariat, and the second the interest of the bourgeoisie ...' (1974: 9). Bettelheim refers to

the '*lack of conformity* between the essentials of the new social relations
. . . and the productive forces . . . which means a certain type of contradiction between the form of property and the real mode of appropria-
tion' (*ibid*.: 23). These are essentially the result of the specific
conjunctures defining the types and numbers of contradictions in a
given social formation.

The Lock/Althusser theses locate the happenings of the 'Stalinian deviation' in the class struggle extant in the USSR. 'A scientific treatment
of the Stalin period will . . . show that the events which characterised it
[trials, purges etc.] were, in spite of "appearances", effects of [a specific]
class struggle fought out in the economic, political and ideological
spheres. . . . The great trials of 1936–38 were not, legally speaking,
directed against the representatives of a particular class, but against
certain senior Party members . . . [and] contained many absurd allega-
tions. But that does not mean that they can be explained – and written off
– as simple "violations of socialist legality". The trials and purges
played a role *determined in the last instance by the class struggle inside the
USSR*, even if in practice their victims were the "wrong" ones' (Lock
1975: 15).

Considered from this viewpoint, the class struggle continued in the
USSR, and Stalin, influenced by '*bourgeois* theory and *bourgeois*
methods' (Lock 1975: 23n), deviated from Marxism both in the 'theoretical' and in the 'political' domains. The Lock/Althusser argument is that
under Stalin the deviation occurred in the ideological and political
spheres and that this did not involve a return to capitalism, but was a
reflection of the class struggle under socialism (see Lock 1975: 23–32).
My criticism of the Althusser/Lock argument is not only that their explanation lacks clarity, but that their analysis of class forces is abstract and
remains unconnected to the class structure of Soviet society. It is a form
of reductionism: conflicts and oppression, by Marxist definition, must
be forms of class struggle.

These authors are heavily dependent in their interpretation on economic analysis, in the sense that at the root of the contradictions and
distortions is the low level of productive forces. Mandel, following
Trotsky, brings out the distinction between the 'non-capitalist mode of
production' and the 'basically bourgeois mode of distribution' (Mandel
1969: 14). Bettelheim emphasises the resolution of conflicts through a
'development of the productive forces which will bring about conformity between social relations and the productive forces themselves'
(1975: 23). Bettelheim quotes Lenin with approval to the effect that in
Russia between 1918 and 1921 there were five different economic

systems or structures – the patriarchal economy, small commodity production, capitalist production, state capitalism and socialism (1975: 17).* These economic structures may well explain some of the contradictions of the first ten years of Soviet power. But, as Bettelheim goes on to argue, the major force is the transition to socialism because the 'predominant orientation' is determined by the 'working class nature of the state' and the state's grasp of the 'commanding heights of the economy' (*ibid.*). Both Bettelheim and Mandel focus on bureaucratic/class forces. Mandel notes the 'severe or extreme forms of bureaucratic deformation and degeneration'. These, he says, are probably not general features of transitional society but are 'in reality peculiarities having less to do with the internal logic of such a society than with the conditions of socio-economic under-development' (1974: 8). From this vantage point, 'the isolation of the October Revolution in an economically under-developed country (with the resulting compulsion to further "primitive socialist accumulation") thereby produced a whole series of distortions from a more mature model of transitional society which were enormously increased by the peculiar development of the subjective factor (the self-identification of the Communist Party of the Soviet Union with the Soviet bureaucracy, the bureaucratisation of the party, Stalinism, etc.)' (*ibid.*).

The emphasis in Mandel's analysis is not on the terror and abrogation of human rights under Stalin denounced by Khrushchev and Medvedev but, following Trotsky, on the betrayal of the international revolution in the policy of 'socialism in one country'. 'It implied a revision of the very concept of world revolution and of its relevance in the imperialist epoch, which in turn entailed a revision of the whole theory of the imperialist epoch' (Mandel 1978: 14). Hence Khrushchev maintained a *continuity* in political practice – that of 'Soviet "national messianism"' and the 'theoretical, political and organisational degeneration which undermined the basis upon which the programme and existence of the Comintern had been founded. . .' (*ibid.*: 15).

The degeneration which occurred in the USSR under Stalin has been cogently analysed by Trotsky (see particularly *The Revolution Betrayed*, 1936). Trotsky saw Stalinism as a consequence of a 'heritage of oppression, misery and ignorance', of the 'cultural level of the country, the social composition of the population, the pressure of a barbaric

*Lenin defined these five elements to be existing in 1918 (*The Tax in Kind*, CW32: 331). In 1919, Lenin identified three 'basic forms of social economy: capitalism, petty commodity production and communism' (*Economics and Politics*, CW30: 108).

world imperialism' ('Stalinizm i bol'shevism', cited by Knei-Paz 1978: 429). Two arguments run through the analysis. First, the low level of the productive forces (in a Marxist sense) gave rise to cultural, economic and political backwardness. The traditional life styles of an uneducated population, the legacy of Tsarist political culture, the low level of political consciousness of the masses as a whole – all these things provided a culture which sustained the degeneration of Stalinism. The low level of productive forces, for instance, led to shortages of necessary commodities and to the distribution of goods and services on bourgeois rather than socialist principles – this was a source of the privileges of the elites. The world view of the masses was still steeped in religion, and the working class – unlike its Western European counterpart – had not absorbed the values of a liberal-democratic bourgeoisie: democracy, freedom of the press, of association, etc. (for an excellent summary of Trotsky's cultural analysis, see Knei-Paz 1978: Chapter 7). Trotsky's second criticism was in terms of bureaucracy. He agreed with Lenin that organisation was necessary and that advanced capitalism did provide the working class with sufficient experience of administration, but he emphasised the fact that the human material utilised by Stalin was backward. Hence his explanation of bureaucracy was not a political one, like Weber's, but was essentially cultural. With higher levels of consciousness on the part of the working class the political power of the Stalinist elites could be constrained. Another conditioning factor, of course, was the absence of the revolution in the advanced West and the lack of commitment by the Stalinist leadership to achieve it.

Unlike Bettelheim, Trotsky and his followers do not reject the categorisation of the contemporary USSR as a workers' state. The USSR is between capitalism and socialism: it is socialist in the sense that it lacks a bourgeois class, which extracts surplus; its economy as a whole is not based on the production of goods for exchange but for use. While politics were dominant under Stalin, the state was dependent on a class basis – the working class – and it was limited in its activity. As Napoleon had destroyed some of the principles of the French Revolution and had nevertheless consolidated bourgeois society, so Stalin – having betrayed the ideals of socialism – had not altered the dominant form of property or type of commodity exchange. Thus Trotsky, while arguing that a socialist form of social relations (in the sense of relations between people) had not been achieved, held that the Soviet Union was socialist in the terms of ownership relations and economic planning.

These criticisms, it seems to me, are fair as far as they go, but they do not adequately integrate a cultural critique into Marxist theory. Also, they do not give sufficient emphasis to a Weberian analysis of power – of the role which incumbency of office or 'professional' position gives to the holder. The Trotskyist explanation of bureaucracy under Stalin is largely cultural in character. It is perhaps instructive to be reminded that Trotsky's own earlier criticism of Party organisation before the Revolution (see p. 51 above) was Weberian in form. I shall return later to include a cultural and a bureaucratic element in my explanation of revolutionary change.

MARXIST CRITIQUES OF BOLSHEVISM

The Marxist approaches we have considered above have all accepted the fundamental positions of Lenin's adaptation of Marxism to Russia. Others do not. Rather paradoxically two opposing schools of thought have arisen implicitly in reaction to Lenin's world view and to Soviet Bolshevism. The first argues that Lenin was a 'voluntarist', putting will above material forces. The second school accuses Lenin of a vulgar materialism and 'determinism' and has sought to develop, on the contrary and on the basis of Marx's writing, a more directly activist theory of 'praxis'.

The first school of thought has a history going back to Lenin's opponents, the Mensheviks, within the Russian Social-Democratic Labour Party and finds expression today among many non-Marxists. The essence of this criticism is that Russia was not ready, in a Marxist sense, for a socialist revolution. In the first place, the material forces were not sufficiently advanced to support a socialist society in advance of capitalism. Knei-Paz points out that Trotsky failed to see Stalinism 'as part of an historical continuum, stretching back to 1903, not 1924' (1978: 437). The notion of permanent revolution, the role of the hegemonic Party, rested for Lenin on the assumption that the working-class revolution would materialise in Western Europe – and this was premature. Hence the Revolution, as a *socialist* revolution had to fail.

In the second place, an ideological superstructure with an advanced Marxist consciousness could not arise from such a basis. We shall return many times to this fundamental criticism of Lenin from quite a diverse range of thinkers. Lenin's philosophy itself, some Marxists have argued, was a bourgeois philosophy which could only legitimate a bourgeois revolution. This thesis has been put trenchantly by Pannekoek and Korsch who argue that Lenin emphasised materialism at the expense of dialectics.

Pannekoek explains Lenin's materialism by reference to Russian conditions in the early twentieth century. The Russian intelligentsia, he argues, was unable to link its activity to a rising commercial and industrial class. To secure the downfall of Tsarism, it allied with social-democracy (Pannekoek 1975: 66). Lenin, then, as a philosopher and activist, argues Pannekoek, had a social role of destroying Tsarism; his philosophy, like Plekhanov's, was 'in accordance' with middle-class materialism (*ibid*.: 86). 'The concordance of Lenin and Plekhanov in their basic philosophical views and their common divergencies from Marx point to their common origins out of Russian social conditions' (*ibid*.: 92). Korsch again reiterates this viewpoint in an article published in Pannekoek's book. He asserts that Lenin's 'revolutionary materialist philosophy' and his 'revolutionary jacobinic politics' hid from him 'the historical truth' that his Russian revolution '. . . was bound to remain a belated successor of the great bourgeois revolutions of the past' (Korsch 1975: 117–18).

The second school of thought again reacts against the results of the October Revolution and the failure of Marxism and Marxist parties to make headway in Western Europe. But this group of thinkers, rather than emphasising the voluntarism of Lenin, sees the degeneration of Marxism arising from an emphasis on the 'objective laws' of nature, which limit human liberty and revolutionary potential. Avineri objects that Lenin (following Engels) had a 'highly mechanistic' view of materialism, and disapproves of consciousness being viewed as a 'reflection of the material, environmental condition of man's existence' (Avineri 1968: 66). Stedman-Jones has highlighted the challenge of a 'romantic scientific thematic' which has been introduced into the thinking of some Marxists, and which provides a critique to the orthodox materialist Marxism of Lenin (Stedman-Jones 1971: 61; he is referring here to Lukacs's *History and Class Consciousness*). This viewpoint has emphasised that a philosophical approach and [that] an attitude of 'cultural radicalism' should inform Western Marxism. As Herf has put it: '[Western Marxism] asserts that the final goals of a free society must be operative in the means toward that goal and that a movement for liberation must prefigure in its forms of organisation and activity a vision of a qualitatively different society' (Herf 1977: 140).

Some critics of Soviet Bolshevism take issue with Lenin's and Trotsky's definition of 'relations to the means of production'. Their definition, for practical purposes (it is argued) refers primarily to classes based on ownership, and this is too narrow, for 'relations to the means of production' should also include social relations in a more general sense. They would include the subordination of workers to management, division of labour, and wage labour. All of these factors, they say, are organically linked to ownership relations to the means of production. The division of labour, it has been argued, is 'the effects' of the capitalist relations to the means of production. One might draw attention to a passage in *The German Ideology* where Marx writes: 'The various stages of development in the division of labour are just so many different forms of ownership, i.e. the existing stage in the division of labour determines also the relations of individuals to one another with reference to the material, instrument and product of labour' (1968: 33). Corrigan, Ramsay and Sayer point out that socialism as developed by the Russian Bolsheviks assumed that the production forces were 'unambiguously technical' and that the material basis for socialism 'was the large-scale machine industry characteristic of "advanced" capitalism'. The implication for policy was that the building of socialism 'becomes theoretically and practically subordinated to the presumed exigencies of a historically unexceptionable path of "modernisation", basic to which is the extension of the division of labour in all its forms' (1978: 30). These writers see as a common recurring theme among Lenin, Trotsky and Stalin an 'economistic view of production'. This developmental strategy limits the Soviet strategy of development. As Fleron has put it: 'it is impossible to instil new class content into organisational forms such as Taylorism that are themselves inherently repressive' (Fleron 1977a: 71). Such writers deplore the legitimation as part of socialism of inequality of income, material incentives, managerial expertise and the utilisation of capitalist techniques (see Corrigan *et al.* 1978: 75). They emphasise the importance of transforming the relations between people by fostering 'the collective and conscious and thus egalitarian self-emancipation of the direct producers, through their own transformation of the social relations within which they produce' (*ibid.*: 51).

Certainly one must concede many of the points made by the above critics. As a form of end state, the social relations described are not 'socialist'. Changing the forms of ownership of the means of production is not sufficient to give rise to socialist relations in its broadest sense. But whether such devices may be a *means* to move to socialism is a more open question. While the USSR under Stalin may have been unduly constrained to adopt more adventurous policies, no socialist state has yet been able to sustain socialist relations in the way advocated by Corrigan, Sayer and Ramsay for any significant length of time. The reversion to a more Soviet type of modernisation in China after Mao is most significant in this respect. One other point that may be made is that the USSR under Stalin did not only copy Western methods, but adopted traditional methods from *pre*-revolutionary Russia which were far from the practices of the advanced states – projects using deported labour had antecedents in Tsarist Russia, and the type of public ownership also bears the imprint of the pre-revolutionary autocracy.

STATE SOCIALISM AS A MODE OF PRODUCTION OR AS A SOCIAL FORMATION?

My discussion of Marxist attempts to characterise Soviet Russia will at least have made it clear that the society born under Lenin and raised by Stalin does not fit neatly the stages of society which Plekhanov and Lenin envisaged. Indeed the concept of the 'mode of production' may not be a very useful term to apply to societies such as the USSR. Hindess and Hirst have put this most clearly when they argue that 'the effectivity of the forces [of production] must induce either a necessary "correspondence" between production and its economic forms or the transformation of those forms because of their non-correspondence.' 'But if mode of production cannot be conceived in terms of determinate "relations of production" on the one hand combined with determinate "forces of production" on the other then the pertinence of the concept "mode of production" within Marxist theory must itself be called into question' (Hindess and Hirst 1977: 54). They go on to suggest that societies that do not fall clearly into one uniquely defined 'mode of production' might be 'displaced by social formation as an object of analysis' (*ibid*.: 55). This provides for a concatenation of economic base, political/legal and ideological-cultural superstructures.

So much time has been wasted in trying to fit Soviet-type societies into categories devised by Marx and Engels but not appropriate to them that perhaps we should accept the advice of Hindess and Hirst and not try. There seems to be general agreement on the part of many commentators that Marx and Engels did not conceive of socialism as a mode of production, but as a transitional phase between modes of production. But the form of the USSR and other societies of this type are more than temporary 'transitional societies'. They have a high degree of permanence and possess the capacity for reproducing themselves. One

91

implication, however, is not merely the description of the Soviet Union as a type of society, but the legitimation of that society as socialist.

It must be conceded that to argue that the USSR is a state socialist mode of production does depart significantly from the ideas of Marx and Engels. Yet this phrase does bring out many differences from the capitalist mode. It is inappropriate, perhaps, because it does not highlight the specific cultural and ideological forms, and the relations between power holders and the masses in these societies. From this point of view, a state socialist social formation – one between capitalism and communism, but something more than elements of both – may be a more apposite term and it does not lead to sterile discussions about whether the contemporary USSR fits categories defined by Marx.

The form of ownership of the means of production as it developed under Stalin was collective, and control of it was exercised by the state. Economic planning involved the exchange of commodities through the medium of money; but such exchange did not involve class exploitation analogous to that of capitalist society; rather it reflected (and still reflects) economic shortages due to the low level of material forces. State socialism is also characterised by recurring sets of relationships in the superstructure – a form of state (widely conceived) to include ideological and repressive apparatuses. Under Stalin there was bureaucratic degeneration: it involved incongruencies between basis and superstructure and between parts of the superstructure. Those who object to the Soviet Union under Stalin being termed 'socialist' do so on many grounds: quite rightly, they point out that many of the practices of Stalin involved the repression of man, that social relations in a general way were not 'socialist'. But to adopt this viewpoint is to conflate communism (or socialism) as a system of economy, and socialism as a 'way of life', as an ideal state.

An analogy may be made with the distinction between capitalism and bourgeois society. Capitalism is a mode of production giving rise to a particular type of superstructure (liberal or parliamentary democracy): typically, this includes certain individual freedoms (of movement, of speech, of assembly and so on), the restraining role of law over the government, a multiple party system, responsibility of the government to the citizen. However, not all forms of capitalism ensure such rights: fascism is a socio-political phenomenon which abrogates nearly all of the individual freedoms and processes of liberal-democratic states. From a Marxist point of view, however, fascism does not transcend the boundaries of capitalism as a mode of production: it is a particular nonliberal, anti-democratic form of the capitalist mode of production.

In the Soviet Union under Stalin, communism as a mode of production was being established, its form of ownership relations might be called 'socialist', its superstructure did not conform with the basis, it combined many forms and practices of Tsarist Russia and advanced capitalism with idealistic attitudes derived from Marxism. Writers on 'socialism' use the term in an ambiguous way: as a mode of production, as a type of ownership relations, as a 'way of life' – including beliefs and sets of ideals in human relations. Here I am defining 'state socialism' as a social formation and 'socialism' as a type of ownership of the means of production: this is not to confuse the term with 'full socialism' or communism as referring to a mode of production superior in all respects to capitalism. As an ideal, as a way of life, the actual processes of Soviet Russia were far from being 'socialistic'.

It must be emphasised that Lenin's and Stalin's views and policies were part of a unique historical period: Soviet Marxism developed in a very backward country which had been isolated from Roman law, and the concepts of individual rights were not developed; the Revolution had also taken place in a hostile capitalist environment. It is perhaps not surprising that the appeal of Soviet Marxism–Leninism is to societies undergoing the early phases of transition to capitalism. For them, Marxism–Leninism provides a praxis of political, economic and social action which is fitting to their needs and enhances their development. Ticktin's view that 'Stalinist-type societies are blind alleys in the world process of the transition towards socialism' (1978: 61) needs amendment. The dynamics of world history show that many countries adopt the Soviet model established under Stalin: it is a model of socialism as development, it is incomplete to regard it as an ideal socialist way of life.

How then can one analyse the state which was constructed under Stalin? Carrillo sums up the objections of many socialists to the Soviet Union when he says that the 'October Revolution has produced a State which is evidently not a bourgeois State, but neither is it as yet the proletariat organised as the ruling class, or a genuine workers' democracy' (1977: 157). This viewpoint, however, even under Stalin, does not invalidate the claim of the Soviet state to be a workers' state. The apparatuses of a state need not be directly administered by its ruling class: capitalists need not and often do not rule directly, but do so through intermediaries who man the state apparatuses – neither the leaders of social-democratic parties when in power, nor the warders in capitalist prisons are strictly 'capitalists'. Hence, if we apply the same logic, it is not as simplistic as many commentators claim, to say that the rulers of a socialist state may rule 'on behalf of' the working class, rather than being at 'the command of' that class.

At the other extreme, it is necessary to guard against a mechanistic interpretation of state and economy, such that ownership relations of the means of production are necessarily extended in a homogeneous way into the groups who control the state apparatus, and their policies become the mere reflection of or, by definition, represent the interests of the working class. Society is structured in a more complex way than that. The state is an instrumentality. Trotsky defined it as follows: 'The state is not an end in itself but is a tremendous means for organising, disorganising and reorganising social relations. It can be a powerful lever for revolution or a tool for organised stagnation, depending on the hands that control it' (1962: 194). The dominant class is itself constituted from various factions which may define interests in different ways; it is also confronted by other groups with values and beliefs remaining from other modes of production – the staff of the bureaucracy, the petty-bourgeois peasant. The state may also be influenced by external powers: the threat of invasion, of economic or financial boycott. 'The state', then, cannot be analysed as being made up of a single institution, being composed of a unitary social group or as an ensemble of interests defining a unique policy for the dominant class. By analogy, in the case of Nazi Germany, a political group was hegemonic which defined the interests of capitalism in a different way from the state power in Britain and the USA. The state must be conceived of as having certain areas of autonomy. Within a given mode of production, there may be many different socio-political formations each giving rise to a unique set of apparatuses. But such apparatuses are limited in one respect: they seek to reproduce the dominant class relations to the means of production established by a given mode of production. Though their policies and personnel differ, capitalist states have one feature in common: they seek to reproduce existing class relations.

In the Soviet Union, the dynamics of the Soviet state under Stalin ensured the reproduction of the relations of man to property as established under Lenin, of the dominant (albeit adapted) ideology of Marxism, of opposition to the leading capitalist states as epitomised under Fascism. The state carried out policies of industrialisation; it developed the material bases of the economy, it increased levels of capital accumulation with surplus product derived from the workers and peasants. This process should not be confused with capitalist development, which was geared to the production of exchange values and profit which accrued to a capitalist class. But the workers did not rule directly. The particular constellation of political forces in power reverted to the style and process of Tsarist Russia; the leader rather than the Party was hegemonic. The demands of the economy – distinguished by its function of accumulation – and the necessity for political homogeneity were rigorously enforced. In institutional terms, the industrial ministries played an important part in defining the priorities of the new Soviet state and helped to displace the hegemonic role of the Party as defined by Lenin. The hostile world environment put a premium on defence, and counter-espionage conditioned the attitude to enemies – real or supposed – of the regime. But for all this, the Party's definition of ownership relations to the means of production remained intact, as did the structure of the economy and process of accumulation. This does not mean that socialism in the sense of a 'way of life' was introduced: Stalinism entailed many horrors (Carrillo: 158; Adler *et al.* 1978). These negative aspects of life in the USSR have been emphasised mostly by Western opponents of Stalinism and it is to these that we now turn.

STALINISM AS TOTALITARIANISM

'Stalinism' is a phenomenon much talked about in the West but it is rarely defined. Tucker points to the difficulty of defining the term: 'such an extreme complex historico-socio-cultural-ideological-personal-political and economic phenomenon as Stalinism, is best simply studied, analysed, described, thought about, interpreted and explained' (Tucker 1977b: 321). This is not a particularly helpful statement because it fails to define specifically what is to be studied, analysed, etc.

In practice, 'Stalinism', as used by most Western writers, is almost synonymous with the notion of 'totalitarianism'. Markovic attempts to define the 'characteristics to be necessary and sufficient conditions of Stalinism':

1. Commitment to a violent anti-capitalist revolution which *does not develop beyond* the replacement of the political power of the bourgeoisie by the power of *political bureaucracy* and of private property by *state ownership* of the means of production.

2. The leading force of the revolution and the backbone of the post-revolutionary society is a *monolithic, strongly-disciplined, strictly hierarchical party* which has a *monopoly* of all economic and political power and *reduces all other* social organisations to its *mere transmissions*.
3. The state tends to exist even after the complete liquidation of a capitalist class. Its primary new function is a *rigid administrative* planning of all production and complete control of all political life. The state is officially a dictatorship of the working class; in reality it is *dictatorship of the party leadership or of one single leader*.
4. The new society is continued as a *collectivist welfare* society in which most forms of *economic and political alienation* would survive.
5. A a consequence of the centralist political and economic structure smaller nations in a multi-national country are *denied self-determination* and continue to be *dominated* by the biggest nation.
6. *All culture is subordinated to the sphere of politics* and is strictly controlled by the ruling party.' (Markovic 1977: 300)

Another definition by Cohen is somewhat more pointed:

Stalinism was not simply nationalism, bureaucratisation, absence of democracy, censorship, police repression and the rest in any precedented sense. These phenomena have appeared in many societies and are rather easily explained.

Instead, Stalinism was excess, extraordinary extremism, in each. It was not, for example, merely coercive peasant policies, but a virtual civil war against the peasantry; not merely police repression, or even civil war style terror, but a holocaust by terror that victimised tens of millions of people for twenty-five years; not merely a Thermidorian revival of nationalist tradition, but an almost fascist-like chauvinism; not merely a leader cult, but deification of a despot. . . . Excesses were the essence of historical Stalinism, and they are what really require explanation (Cohen 1977: 12–13)

Alvin Gouldner defines Stalinism as 'a systematic regime of terror aimed at bringing about a property transfer, where private property (used for productive purposes) is supplanted by state property. . . . Stalinism is a reign of terror aiming at the collectivisation of property, where the surrogate of the collective group to whom the property is transferred is the state' (Gouldner 1978: 10–11).

Roy Medvedev (citing L. El'konin) summarises what he calls 'Stalinist pseudosocialism' as:

The cult of the state and worship of rank, the irresponsibility of those who hold power and the population's lack of rights, the hierarchy of privileges and the canonization of hypocrisy, the barrack system of social and intellectual life, the suppression of the individual and the destruction of independent thought, the environment of terror and suspicion, the atomisation of people and the notorious 'vigilance', the uncontrolled violence and the legalised cruelty. (Medvedev 1971: 553)

Solzhenitsyn is yet another and a dramatic interpreter of the Stalin era in a totalitarian vein. His works centre on the Soviet Union as a prison: society is a gigantic prison camp. (Adler *et al.* (1978) estimate that 10 million died in the camps in the 1930s.) The population is enslaved, it is not subject to law; symbolically those in the camps are repressed but have committed no crime. Stalinism is essentially the imposition of arbitrary rule; it is a tyranny enslaving man.

It is important to note that all these descriptions are selective of certain aspects of Soviet reality under Stalin. They emphasise the dominant and uncontrolled power of the repressive state apparatus. These definitions focus attention on the coercive and dictatorial side of Stalin's rule and they remind us of the considerable social, personal and individual costs paid in the USSR to 'build socialism'. These interpretations, however, are not adequate descriptions as they deal only with certain facets of life under Stalin. They are moralistic in tone and, while a cruel tyranny must be morally condemned, such condemnation does not as such provide any analysis of the causes of events or the relationships between various antecedents and their outcomes. Denunciations (or eulogies) of Stalin do not provide us with any theoretical underpinnings with which to analyse the impact of revolution. Also one cannot make adequate moral judgements of societies unless one is aware of the intentions of their leaders, of the alternative courses of action available and of the balance between good and evil. 'Stalinism', so defined, is a partial analysis and the emphasis on coercion, on 'excesses', on terror, has to be seen in the context of political goals, Russian traditions, industrialisation, cultural change and the world political context.

To restrict one's account of totalitarianism to its emotive use would be to underestimate an important explanation of Soviet society. Totalitarianism as a sociological concept involves the politicisation of society directly and indirectly through the agency of the state; it entails the direction of the economy and control over other social institutions, such as the family. Many commentators attempt to link the authoritarian political rule of Stalin (and its positive and negative effects) to political goals and objectives of Bolshevism; others bring out the Russian cultural context.

Stalin's Bolshevism: legitimation and critique

Unlike many Marxist critiques of the Soviet Union, which see Stalin as being a deviation away from Lenin, theorists of totalitarianism argue for a continuity between these two leaders and posit Lenin as the creator of totalitarianism. Robert Conquest regards Lenin as a Blanquist and defines 'that essential of the Lenin concept' as 'the idea of transforming society from above by authoritarian means' (Conquest 1972: 132–3). As Kolakowski has put it: Lenin was the 'creator of totalitarian doctrine and of the totalitarian state in embryo' (Kolakowski 1978: vol. 3,3).

One of the clearest statements of continuity between Lenin and Stalin has been provided by Alfred Meyer. 'Stalinism can and must be defined as a pattern of thought and action that flows directly from Leninism. Stalin's way of looking at the world, his professed aims, the decisions he made at variance with one another, his conceptions of the tasks facing the communist state – these and many specific traits are entirely Leninist. . . . The decisions made by Stalin and the manner in which they were made and executed were prepared by Lenin. His stress on the primacy of the party and the power struggle, his preoccupation with problems of economic construction and cultural transformation, his readiness to manipulate men and institutions, his faith in organisation, and his ruthlessness in implementing policies – in all these traits Stalin has trod in Lenin's footsteps' (Meyer 1957: 782–3). Alvin Gouldner has taken a similar line on continuity: 'the essence of both Leninism and Stalinism then was precisely this fusion of a relatively voluntaristic politics with a model of economic development that stressed industrial development seen as a matter of fostering technological hardware (e.g. "electrification") and the "forces of production"' (Gouldner 1978: 38).

What then was the intent of the revolution that Stalin carried out? Gouldner emphasises the centrality of collectivisation. The regime of terror perpetrated by a personal dictatorship through a bureaucracy was instrumental in bringing about '*a mass property transfer*' (Gouldner 1978: 12n). Gouldner does not see 'socialism in one country' as particularly novel to Stalin and opposed to Bolshevism. He cites Lenin in 1921 as saying that 'socialism in an isolated Soviet Russia was possible' (p.25). He points out that the leading Bolsheviks (Lenin, Bukharin and Stalin) 'had thus all been converging on a policy whose common dimension was socialism in one country. In that sense, Stalin was correct in holding that socialism in one country was "Leninist"' (p. 25). As with Medvedev's account, the punitive actions of the Soviet government are stressed by Gouldner, but he sees them as conditioned by the need to assert the hegemony of an 'urban-centered power elite' over the countryside; there occurred then 'an internal colonialism' which mobilised state power against 'colonial tributaries in rural territories' (p.13). The Bolsheviks, according to Gouldner, were faced by a hostile 'peasant community' which had for centuries 'remained largely solidary against the outside and the city' (p. 21). This internal colonialism was based on a 'Leninist voluntarism' which stemmed from Lenin's views of *What is to be Done?* – 'socialism and socialist consciousness have to be brought to groups from the outside by a theoretically prescient elite . . .' (p. 26). Terror was utilised to carry out these goals.

Gouldner's analysis does not identify any *class* conflict in Soviet society. He alleges that Trotsky, in defining the class character of the Soviet Union in terms of the 'ownership' of the means of production, 'Fails to weigh the significant distinction between ownership and control' (p.9), but he does not provide any linkages between the bureaucracy, extraction of surplus and class rule. While he rightly points to the conditioning role of the Bolsheviks' 'special reading of Marxism, i.e. "scientific socialism"' (p.46), he fails to understand that this had a class orientation. He characterises the 'property transfer' in political and cultural terms – the 'great' and 'little' traditions – and the cleavage as being between town and country (pp. 13–18). While this is important it is also necessary to distinguish how far interests of 'town' and 'country' represented class conflicts.

Knei-Paz in his treatise on Trotsky regards the rise of totalitarianism to be 'rooted not only in the conditions of the October Revolution but in the very aspirations of the latter' (1978: 435). Knei-Paz regards the 'cornerstone of political legitimacy and action' to be in the dictatorship of the proletariat and the one-party system. The ideology of Marxism–Leninism remained the 'criterion for pronouncing upon the legitimacy of private and public behaviour' (*ibid.*).

Stalin, from this line of argument, carried out a social and economic revolution. Given the economic and political conditions – the low level of productive forces, popular resistance – trials, purges and terror were crucial. Knei-Paz points out that political violence prevented 'peripheral focuses of political power from forming – in the party, the army, even the bureaucracy – and thus pulling in a direction other than that decreed by the economic revolution' (1978: 436). Far from being a Thermidor identified with conservatism and stabilisation, Stalin carried out a programme of fundamental changes, the necessity of which had been agreed by Lenin and Trotsky.

Other Western writers, particularly historians, attempting to generalise about the impact of revolution, have identified many factors which have favoured *continuity* between the past and post-revolutionary developments. Two variations of this approach may be distinguished: first, that which emphasises the way that the *revolutionary* transformation which occurred under Stalin was linked to pre-revolutionary conditions: an example of this school is R. C. Tucker. Second are those writers who bring out the ways that the intentions of the revolutionaries were *limited* by the forces of tradition: here we shall consider E. H. Carr and Roger Pethybridge.

R. C. Tucker has provided one of the most sophisticated analyses of continuity of revolution under Stalin. Though he disagrees with Meyer's interpretation of Stalinism flowing 'directly from Leninism', he sees Leninism as 'an important contributory factor' (1977b: 78). Tucker makes three points concerning the maintenance, in the Stalin epoch, of the revolutionary process started by Lenin and the Bolsheviks. First, Stalinism was 'a revolutionary phenomenon in essence'. Second, it was an 'integral phase of the Russian revolutionary process' carried out from above. Third, notable among the factors explaining the form it took are 'the heritage of Bolshevik revolutionism, the heritage of old Russia, and the mind and personality of Stalin' (1977b: 78). Hence Tucker replaces Medvedev's personality explanation with an essentially culturalist one. The dominant *Soviet* culture was made up of a Marxist–Leninist ideology, the structure of government, political procedures and education, amongst other things (see Tucker 1977b: 80). Like Gouldner, Tucker contrasts this with the rural traditional culture: 'a Russia of churches, the village *mir*. The patriarchal peasant family, old values, old pastimes, old outlooks . . .' (*ibid.*) Stalinism was a process which broke the old order to its foundations, this was carried out by the 'rural revolution' – mass collectivisation – which accompanied the industrial revolution (Tucker 1977b: 82).

The industrial and agricultural revolutions, argues Tucker, are a continuation of Lenin's 'revolutionary leadership' (*ibid.*: 90). Citing Lenin, he says, 'The dictatorship of the proletariat is the *continuation* of the class struggle in *new* forms' (*ibid.*). Collectivisation, then, was a continuation of the internal class struggle; and Stalin had the support of many Bolsheviks who had grown up during War Communism. The situation of grain shortage, the internal and external threat, and the reaction of the Bolshevik leaders were conditioned by the heritage of revolutionary War Communism political culture (*ibid*.: 89–93). Tucker's argument, however, is more than a simple extrapolation of Civil War political culture into later times. It involves 'a reversion to a revolutionary process seen earlier in Russian history' (*ibid*.: 95). Stalin's 'socialism differed from that of Marx, Engels and Lenin: it involved mass poverty, sharp stratification, constant fear, national chauvinism, and state powers'. It is these elements that had a pre-history in the political culture of Russian tsarism; it existed as a pattern in the Russian past and hence *could* be seen by a twentieth-century statesman as both a precedent and legitimation of a political course that would, in essentials, recapitulate the historical pattern' (*ibid*.: 95).

One can draw parallels between industrialisation motivated by defence needs under Peter the Great and under Stalin. Also the *collective* farm was similar in many aspects to the pre-revolutionary commune: the *kolkhoznik* was 'bound' to the farm in a way similar to that in which the serf has been to the *mir*. The use of forced labour for collective projects was also a pre-revolutionary practice, albeit then on a smaller scale. The political process of Stalinism could be interpreted as a reversion in a new guise to the 'binding of all classes . . . in compulsory service to the state' (Tucker 1977b: 99). As we saw earlier, Stalin legitimated an important role for the state under socialism. The cultural dimension was reflected in the personality of Stalin – culture, for Tucker, is 'something which has its being mainly *within* people' (*ibid*.: 103). A comparison between the Petrine and Bolshevik Revolutions has been well put by Berdyaev. 'They display the same barbarity, violence, forcible application of certain principles from above downwards, the same rupture of organic development, and repudiation of tradition, the same etatism, hypertrophy of government, the same formation of a privileged bureaucratic class, the same centralization, the same desire sharply and radically to change the type of civilization' (Berdyaev 1937: 10).

The second version of the continuity thesis mentioned above, concerns the *limitations* which the historical context stamps on the pursuit of revolutionary goals, and the ways in which the forces of tradition have subsequently modified the goals of the leaders of the Revolution. De Tocqueville emphasised the continuity involved in the French Revolution and E. H. Carr and R. Pethybridge, to take but two examples, have built on this basis in their interpretation of 'the legacy of history', to use Carr's words (Carr 1958: Ch. 1).* Such analysis is deductive and follows empirical study of the course of revolution. Let me briefly indicate what these two authors have identified in their quest to analyse 'the tension between change and continuity' (Carr 1958: 4), or, as Pethybridge depicts it, 'the tension between theory and reality' (1974:8).

In a rather general way, Carr points to the limiting factors of 'a specific material environment' of men 'reared in a specific national tradition'; to the changing role of a revolutionary theory and practice when it becomes 'the theory and practice of government'; to the practical obligations to conduct foreign relations of some kind with other states (*ibid.*: 4–6). The new incumbents of power faced similar 'basic geographical and economic factors' as their forebears. The wide territory, grim climatic conditions and unfavourable distribution of resources were constraints for Bolsheviks as they had been for the Tsars. Carr goes on to link the development of Bolshevik ideology *before* the Revolution to Russian conditions: the form of Party organisation described in *What is to be Done?*, the link with the Narodniks, the peasantry as a revolutionary force – the Bolsheviks were considered to be 'Slavophilising Marxists' (*ibid.*: 17). Carr, somewhat similarly to Tucker, sees Stalin's declaration of 'Socialism in one country' as an amalgam of revolutionary, though 'russified' Marxism and the 'familiar features of the Russian landscape and the Russian outlook' (*ibid.*: 21–2).

This approach has been applied in a more ambitious and detailed manner by Roger Pethybridge. He attempts to explain the non-implementation of specific pre-revolutionary Leninist policies after 1917: he considers 'the reverberation of certain Bolshevik political and social ideas against the sounding board of Soviet social realities' (1974: 7). It is in this process that Pethybridge believes that the essential nature of Stalinism may be examined. The explanation for the eventual drift to a totalitarian system is to be found in the 'creeping and uncongenial effects of social backwardness. . . . The pre-existing social forces may not have played an active, dynamic role in politics after 1917, [but] they did have a deep and lasting negative influence on the attainment of Bolshevik social, economic and political goals' (1974: 13, 15).

A thread which runs through his argument is the resolution of the tensions between Leninist theory and Soviet reality which led to the

---

* Stephen White has adopted a similar approach in stressing the continuity between the political culture of autocratic Russia and contemporary Soviet society (White 1979: 64–5, 167).

epoch of Stalinism (p. 8), Pethybridge's basis for the selection of social facts is not clearly specified. He argues that 'it is pointless to use a theory as the criterion for the selection of the relevant facts and then on the basis of those facts to illustrate and confirm the theory by which they have been chosen. . . . Social history . . . must apply to society as a whole, from which nothing can be excluded' (p. 2). This methodological approach, of course, does not exclude the selection of themes and topics which define the set of social facts which are uncovered by the researcher and welded by him or her into an historical explanation. In historical as in all social research, some assumptions about cause and effect or about interaction between persons, institutions, social forces, values, culture and so on, are made. The attempt to make explicit or to codify is a theoretical activity. And Pethybridge's own work is more than an attempt to fill in gaps left by other writers. In his view, 'Soviet social and political life in the years 1917–1929 was not completely incoherent' (*ibid.*), he then goes on to state his own theory of society. 'Like Soviet society itself [social and political life] contained many semi-organised parts with interconnecting influences. But no total order is evident, so that ties between topics . . . cannot be rigidly defused nor rendered all embracing. Any attempt to do this would be to fall into the trap of imagining, together with Soviet Marxist historians, that social reality can be completely structured, or that a part of it can regulate all the rest. This would imply that there can be only one correct sociological theory' (p. 12). But Pethybridge here is arguing that this structurally determined theory is incorrect and that Soviet society operated with some units having more or less semi-autonomous existence.

Pethybridge defines five attitudes to policy by Lenin and the Bolsheviks: to transform deep-rooted institutions like the family; to dismantle the standing army; to inculcate deep culture through education; to impose large-scale social and economic forms of life; to abolish bureaucracy (p. 8). And he attempts to show how these various attitudes were thwarted after the Revolution. (I say 'attitudes' because the Bolsheviks in many cases had no specific policies in relation to these subjects.) Let us list the detailed reasons Pethybridge puts forward to explain the gap between the expectations and the actual performance of the Bolsheviks. I have attempted here to abstract these explanations from the empirical discussion in order to analyse Pethybridge's assumptions about the impact of revolution.

There are four different types of explanations of the changes in Bolshevik policy and these are documented in Pethybridge's account.

First, there are those that see Bolshevik ideology itself as compounded, or influenced by, non-Marxist sources. There is a Russian cultural component in the ideology of Bolshevism. Examples here are that the Old Bolsheviks were 'the direct intellectual and social heirs of a prominent section of Russia's pre-revolutionary intelligentsia' (p. 27). Social backwardness influenced 'the authoritarian elements in the Leninist political model' (p. 22) and Lenin's theory of Party organisation was in the Russian tradition. The Bolsheviks, says Pethybridge, clung to the authoritarian wing of the utopian tradition, the rigid autocracy gave rise to rigid theories to counter it (p. 28). Lenin also took over in practice the Tsarist conception of local government – state politics prevailed over local politics (p. 266). Family reform, particularly as postulated by the Left Communists, was also inspired by non-Bolshevik ideology (p. 46). These two examples point to the essential ambiguity of Leninist policy: it contained anti-bureaucratic participatory sentiments derived from Marx, but was itself bureaucratic and elitist. In terms of family policy, it contained at the same time libertarian views as well as Marxist ones. Changes in policy after 1917 were to some extent shifts between different components of Bolshevism.

Second, there are the relatively autonomous social forces which the Bolsheviks had to control and which were either strong enough to deflect Bolshevik policy or were absorbed into policy. The major factor here is the social underdevelopment of Russia for socialist revolution. Such underdevelopment is manifested in many ways: by the large peasant population – 'this heavy millstone [of the peasantry] made the Bolsheviks adjust their policies on every issue' (p. 15); by poor communications, especially illiteracy; by the psychological predisposition of the population; by its lack of initiative inherited from the Tsarist system – 'It was not possible in psychological terms to turn a worker conditioned by Tsarist factory life into a self-reliant administrator overnight' (p. 276). The social inadequacy of the working class was part of the reason why workers' control failed; and the low standard of literacy and education and the incapacity of the proletariat led to the 'reintroduction of bureaucracy' (p. 57). In this respect, Pethybridge has Lenin to support him. In *Better Fewer, but Better*, Lenin pointed out that 'These defects [of the state apparatus] are rooted in the past which, although it has been overthrown, has not yet been overcome, has not yet reached the state of a culture that has receded into the distant past. . . . It could not be otherwise in a revolutionary epoch, when development proceded at such breakneck speed that in a matter of five years we passed from Tsarism to the Soviet system' (*SW*3: 829–30) Lenin called for the abolition of 'the cruder types of pre-bourgeois culture' which prevailed, i.e. 'bureaucratic culture' and 'serf-culture' (*SW* 3: 829).

Thirdly, there are the political limitations of a revolutionary seizure of power – albeit carried out with the use of coercion by the Bolsheviks. These range from the constant constraints of geography, climate, economic resources, to the incapacity of the revolution to extend itself over certain areas of social life. Pethybridge quotes De Tocqueville approvingly when he points out that the French Revolution changed the form of government and 'decapitated' the administration, but left the 'trunk of the administration' untouched (p. 278). Officials in administration tend to practise 'habitual' activity (p. 280) and essentially political revolutions do not penetrate below the upper echelons of state administrations. Another example is to be found in the traditional forms of peasant life: this is largely (not entirely) a self-regulating economy of the barter type (pp. 199–200), and rural traditional institutions such as the *dvor*, *mir* and *skhod* continued into the post-revolutionary period in the main uninfluenced by Soviet power and promoted views hostile to the revolutionaries (p. 212). The mores of the peasant family were a 'fourth pillar' to the official creed of Autocracy (p. 49). The October Revolution was largely an urban revolution and the dichotomy between town and village continued (pp. 199–200).

Fourthly, there were factors which were directly caused by the Revolution itself. These included the emigration of many of the professional and intellectual classes, groups which would normally play a crucial part in industrial development (p. 219). Their absence entailed upward mobility of peasants and workers. Such mobility, argues Pethybridge, gave rise, on the one hand, to loyalty to the regime of previously politically excluded masses (p. 304), but also created, on the other, a sense of insecurity in those cut off from their traditional roots. The new political elites were highly motivated to stay in power (p. 67): the use of force, of the police, was directed to this goal. Pethybridge argues that the minority support of the communists turned an authoritarian system into a totalitarian one (p. 256). The post-revolutionary regime was not 'situation-determined' but was partly created by the wills of the incumbents of power: to some extent, at least, the political elites willed the society to become totalitarian (p. 307). But the political elite in turn was influenced by the strata who benefited from Stalin's rule. By 1936, the 'Soviet intelligentsia' was ten million strong. These men influenced policy. And one must agree with the review of R. W. Davies that studies of Stalin have underestimated 'the influence in the party and on Stalin, of those party members who eagerly supported him' (Davies 1979: 9). The study of such influence is an area of Soviet life little studied because Westerners have been totally occupied with the leader. Kemp-Welch, in considering the intellectual order of Stalinism, has argued that much policy initiative originated 'from below': in the field of intellectual life, 'party officials of lower rank felt bold enough to initiate policy changes on their own and to push proposals upwards as a conscious act of insubordination to their immediate superiors' (1978: 8). This approach is also somewhat at variance with Pomper's view that 'historical environments do not control human development in a one-way causality, since the various psychologies of leadership are shaped in the happenstance of individual biographies and carried forward to their various intersections with history' (1978: 29). It seems to me to to be more true to say that there are sub-cultures which 'reach down' to the leadership from society and these are important conditioning features of leadership styles.

These four factors seem to me to contain most of the crucial influences limiting the course of the Revolution and bring out the complexity of the impact of revolution in its historical perspective. This does not mean that analyses such as Pethybridge's should go without challenge. The libertarian elements in Lenin's *State and Revolution* may not, for instance, represent a possible course of action in the immediate post-revolutionary period; Lenin's views on workers' control may not have changed very significantly with the course of revolution. The political significance of revolution as a means of social and economic change which is not considered favourably (pp. 67,240) may also be queried. As Tucker has pointed out, there was continuity of a revolutionary type which stemmed from pre-1917 Russia. In the work of Carr, Pethybridge, Tucker and Knei-Paz, while still retaining a totalitarian model, we have more emphasis on Soviet history and on explanation, and the denunciatory element does not obtrude. This approach, however, tends to neglect class factors made prominent by Marxists.

SOME CONCLUSIONS: EXPLANATIONS OF REVOLUTIONARY CHANGE AND CULTURAL CONTINUITY

The explanations of the impact of revolution considered above have been both illuminating and, as they stand, inadequate. The chief advantage of the more traditional Marxist interpretation is that it does focus on the class character of the October Revolution; whatever one may say about the level of productive forces, there occurred a change of class relations; and the development of the economic basis (both industrial and agricultural) would appear to be a continuation of the industrial revolution. The notion of a social formation is also valuable in accommodating activities in the superstructure which were 'incongruent' with the dominant mode of production. It is at this point that Marxist explanation breaks down and sometimes denunciation of the Stalinist order of things takes pride of place in the writing of Marxist and radical critics of Stalin.

Those who argue the case of cultural continuity throw much light on the conditioning forces of Stalin's Russia. Writers such as Pethybridge bring out the fact that various social institutions, such as the family, provided a greater level of 'resistance' to the political sector, to social ideals, and to the arrangements that the polity sought to enforce. The implications here are more serious for the advocates of revolution as a mechanism of change, for it stresses that there are limits to revolution and it casts doubt on the concept of 'totalness' of revolutionary change. This argument in limiting the powers of those in authority also applies against those who argue the 'totalitarian' case. Cultural determinists, such as Tucker, stress the other side of the cultural dimensions: the continuity of *revolutionary* forms from Tsarist Russia. A point that I have laboured earlier is that Soviet Marxism–Leninism was a product of Russian culture, different from that of Western European Marxism. Stalin carried forward that tradition and adapted it to the circumstances of an encircled and backward Soviet state. Stalin and his Bolshevik associates were also heirs of a Tsarist tradition and such forces of continuity undoubtedly affected the style and process of politics.

A fault of those who emphasise the 'cult of personality' is that they take too narrow a standpoint, pinpointing the degeneration of the USSR on Stalin and a number of his cronies. A more correct explanation would be to locate personality in a Russian cultural context and to emphasise the conditioning effects of Russian and early Soviet history on the men who ruled Russia. The outlook of Stalin had much in common with that of Lenin: the analysis of modes of production, the effects of base on superstructure, the dictatorship of the proletariat, the notion of a Rousseauean form of state and Party leadership are crucial components of Lenin's and Stalin's practice. To use an analogy from Stalin's essay on linguistics: the grammar of Bolshevism remained the same, but the vocabulary changed. The Russian leaders took for granted their own history and culture and looked to it for lessons in how to solve their problems: a population bound to the service of the state was one of their solutions. Barbarous methods were used to fight Russian barbarism.

But from a Marxist position the post-revolutionary class structure was transformed: individual rights to property were severely curtailed. Soviet Russia was not a capitalist Russia; in a Marxist sense, it remained transitionary, combining state property with forms of distribution similar to, though not as extreme as, those of bourgeois society.

The approaches of Marxists and culturalists must be combined to explain the impact of Revolution. Social change must be considered to be compounded of various types of movement and a political revolution is an attempt to establish a new threshold for a limited number of such types of change. As Ward has put it: 'Usually one thinks of a revolution as one event or at least one interconnected series of events. But we are in fact living with ten or twenty such revolutions' (Ward 1962: 13, cited by Wolf 1976: 77). Unless there is a coincidence of relatively independent energies in the various sectors of society (personality, polity, economy) or unless such change can be effected, then a societal revolution does not occur, and change remains essentially limited. Hence to achieve a complete *socialist* revolution, the impetus for change must be congruent in several sectors. The political seizure of power by the Bolsheviks in 1917, and its political and social consolidation by Stalin were important 'moments' in the socialist revolutionary process. To ensure socialism as a 'way of life', as well as an 'economic basis', socialist ideals must dominate in the patterns of values and beliefs which men and women have internalised. But Stalinist Russia did not achieve socialism in this sense. As the French Revolution ushered in the Napoleonic dictatorship and as bourgeois-democratic rights of suffrage have not been achieved in most European countries until the twentieth century, the process of revolution must be seen as a drawn out sequence of changes. As 1789 was a decisive moment in the rise of capitalism in France, so was 1917 a crucial step to socialism in Russia. One of the most important conditioning and limiting factors in Stalin's Russia, was that the stock of personalities (both among leaders and masses) had not absorbed such ideals; and the Russian revolutionary struggle which culminated in the October Revolution was fought against Tsarism as much as, if not more than, against capitalism. Stalin, then, continued the Revolution begun by Lenin: but it has remained an incomplete revolution and many of its features have been, and remain, traditional and Russian. In the next chapter, I shall attempt to combine the strengths of both the cultural and Marxist approaches in one model.

4

wwwwwwwwwwwwwwwwwwwwwwwwwwwwwwwwwwwwwwwwwwwwwwwwwwwwwwwwwwwwwwwwww

A paradigm of revolution and social change

A FRAMEWORK OF ANALYSIS

In foregoing chapters we have considered the evolution of Marxism–Leninism as a legitimating ideology and some of the interpretations of developments in the Soviet Union under Stalin. All these interpretations, from one point of view or the other, have been found inadequate and here our task is to generalise about the impact of revolution from the experience of Soviet Russia. I shall attempt to combine the strengths of historical materialism with the paradigm of Talcott Parsons, who has been aptly described as attempting to develop an 'understanding of the formal structure of multi-dimensional causality and value internalisation into a fully elaborated theory of social life' (Alexander 1978: 183). Rather than seeing Marxism and structural functionalism as dramatically opposed theories of society, I see them as being in many ways complementary. As was pointed out above in Chapter 1 (p. 12), Lenin's is a functional rather than a causal theory. While some Marxists have recognised the functional component in Marxist analysis (G. A. Cohen and Sztompka are notable), this analysis has not been applied, except somewhat crudely, to state socialist society. Also, the system categorisation of Parsons, which I believe to be useful for at least heuristic purposes, has not been readily appreciated by writers on socialist states.

The lack of interest in the phenomenon of revolution by Parsonian theorists and the disdain for the alleged inherent conservatism of structural functionalism by Marxists has led to an impoverishment of the study of the revolutionary process. From the discussion in the earlier chapters of this book, it is clear that to account adequately for the revolutionary process attention must be focussed on: the class system, culture, the stocks of personality and the structural components of society itself (goals, forms of integration of government and of economy). To give full weight to these factors the insights of both Marx and Parsons have to be employed. What follows is a preliminary attempt. As the Parsonian system is not common currency among historians, sociologists and political scientists, a brief explanation may be necessary. Before considering the analysis of a 'society', we may examine the concepts of culture and personality.

Culture and personality may be considered *analytically* as systems* independent of a society: of course, any given society has a cultural dimension and a stock of personalities and we shall turn to discuss this later. A culture may be defined as a system 'organised around the characteristics of complexes of symbolic meaning – the codes in terms of which they are structured, the particular clusters of symbols they employ, and the conditions of their utilization, maintenance and change as parts of action systems' (Parsons 1971: 5). Cultural systems include ideas and beliefs, expressive symbols and value orientations (Parsons and Shils 1951: 21). Culture includes language, science, systems of belief, and such artefacts may exist independently of a society: the culture of Ancient Greece or the Middle Ages is preserved in books; similarly, religions and philosophies may be considered analytically apart from the societies in which they were created.

The personality system is made up of the 'orientation of action of *any one* given actor and its attendant motivational processes' (Parsons and Shils 1951: 7); personality is the 'organised system of orientation and motivation to the *internalisation* of values'. These patterns of internalisation may be derived from the cultural system, but they are not identical with it. Parsons suggests that one might 'in a very abstract sense' define in a society a 'modal personality type' given by the societal value system (Parsons and Bales 1956: 159). It is important to emphasise that any given real person will not have such personality characteristics, and that actual patterns of behaviour cannot simply be derived from this modal type. But the 'modal personality type' points to predispositions which will influence persons' reactions to external stimuli or events.

Parsons has suggested that one may differentiate between four generic types of situationally generalised goals which may be predominant. These are: 'success' or achievement goals, 'hedonistic' or gratification goals, personality, integrative or 'satisfaction' goals, and 'creative'

---

* Parsons also includes the behavioural organism; this is of little interest to the present discussion and is ignored.

or accomplishment goals (Parsons and Bales 1956: 177). Culture and personality may be regarded as analytical systems which are 'external' to society, they are environments which condition it. Let us now turn to look at how Parsons conceives of a society.

A society for Parsons is one special type of social system: it is 'characterised by the highest level of self-sufficiency relative to its environments including other social systems' (Parsons 1971: 8). A society in turn may be analysed into four sub-systems: the maintenance of institutionalised cultural patterns (socialisation), the societal community (the integrative aspects), the polity, and the economy. These are given the symbols L, I, G, A. A society must solve four problems: these are what Parsons calls the functions of pattern maintenance and tension management (L), integration (I), goal attainment (G), and adaptation (A). For Parsons pattern maintenance is the process by which the culture of a society is internalised by the individual personalities through their socialisation. Integration has to do with maintaining the wholeness of the system; social control provides mechanisms by which order and integration are maintained. Goal attainment is the co-operative effort required to fulfil certain general objectives for the society. Adaptation is primarily concerned with the adjustment of society to the physical environment, with role differentiation and the division of labour.

In the analysis of society, Parsons has been concerned with the nature of exchange between these functional components. He regards societies to be in a kind of moving equilibrium. Exchange takes place between the four sub-systems of a society as in Figure 1 (Parsons 1963: 262). Here we see the four functional components: the economy A, the polity G, law and social control I, culture and motivational commitments L. The six sets of arrows illustrate the double exchange of products between each pair of sub-systems. (Further explanation see Rocher 1974: 63–7.) Taking one exchange as an example (A–G), Parsons conceives of this relationship as the 'resource mobilization system'. The economy (A) is concerned with the control of productive resources; the polity (G), however, performs the important role of creating the conditions or the 'opportunity for effectiveness' – it allocates, for instance, capital and it creates levels of credit. The economy in turn provides services (such as employment) to meet societal goals. A more detailed description of the exchanges between all four sub-systems is given in Figure 2.

Let me draw attention to two components of the model. First, we may note that at any level of analysis no single unit monopolises the exchange transactions between the structures constituting the

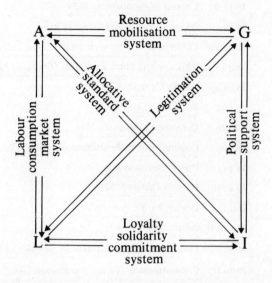

A   Adaptive sub-system
       (the economy)

G   Goal attainment sub-system
       (the polity)

I   Integrative sub-system
       (law [as norms] and
       social controls)

L   Pattern-maintenance
       (locus of cultural and
       motivational commitments)

1. Format of the societal interchange system
   (Diagram based on Parsons 1963:262.)

functional sub-systems. Parsons is aware that the exchanges as shown in the diagram may not correspond to all empirical cases, but he maintains that the transactions tend towards equilibrium: 'The system involving these transactions is a balancing system, subject to conditions of equilibrium' (Parsons 1959: 17) and he refers to his scheme as 'the analysis of dynamic equilibrating processes' (1959: 36.* Parsons therefore follows one of his mentors, Alfred Marshall, in regarding the

---

* As Blain (1971: 682) has pointed out, the actual operation of the Parsonian exchange system results in a large number of interchanges (he calculates 192 or 768, if interchanges are double). But this does not by itself lead one to reject the Parsonian system; the complexity of the model is a reflection of the complexity of the social order.

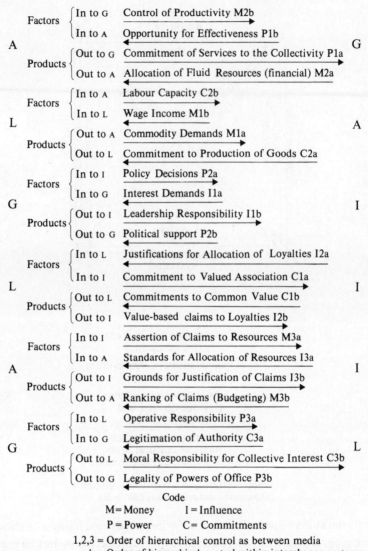

A

Factors
{ In to G — Control of Productivity M2b
{ In to A — Opportunity for Effectiveness P1b

Products
{ Out to G — Commitment of Services to the Collectivity P1a
{ Out to A — Allocation of Fluid Resources (financial) M2a

G

L

Factors
{ In to A — Labour Capacity C2b
{ In to L — Wage Income M1b

Products
{ Out to A — Commodity Demands M1a
{ Out to L — Commitment to Production of Goods C2a

A

G

Factors
{ In to I — Policy Decisions P2a
{ In to G — Interest Demands I1a

Products
{ Out to I — Leadership Responsibility I1b
{ Out to G — Political support P2b

I

L

Factors
{ In to L — Justifications for Allocation of Loyalties I2a
{ In to I — Commitment to Valued Association C1a

Products
{ Out to L — Commitments to Common Value C1b
{ Out to I — Value-based claims to Loyalties I2b

I

A

Factors
{ In to I — Assertion of Claims to Resources M3a
{ In to A — Standards for Allocation of Resources I3a

Products
{ Out to I — Grounds for Justification of Claims I3b
{ Out to A — Ranking of Claims (Budgeting) M3b

I

G

Factors
{ In to L — Operative Responsibility P3a
{ In to G — Legitimation of Authority C3a

Products
{ Out to L — Moral Responsibility for Collective Interest C3b
{ Out to G — Legality of Powers of Office P3b

L

Code

M = Money   I = Influence
P = Power   C = Commitments

1,2,3 = Order of hierarchical control as between media
a,b = Order of hierarchical control within interchange systems

'In' means Input of a category of resources to the sub-system
        indicated from the other member of the pair
'Out' means Output of a category of 'product' from the indicated
        source to the relevant destination
Every double interchange consists of one input (factor)
        interchange and one output (product) interchange

2. Categories of societal interchange

Reprinted by permission from the Proceedings of the American Philosophical Society VOL 107, NO. 3 (1962).

Source: Parsons 1963:263.

optimum condition (under the conditions of a frêe and perfect market) to be at the point of equilibrium. In practice, equilibrium is seldom reached and disequilibrium occurs; however, as in neo-classical economics, there is an assumption that oscillation occurs around theoretical equilibrium points. Parsons's ideal paradigm may be regarded as the sociological equivalent of Marshall's perfect competition model of the economy. Also Parsons had made explicit the occurrence of 'deflation' and 'inflation' in politics and in economics (1959: 19), these being deviations, as it were, away from equilibrium.

In an evolutionary sense, if certain conditions are *not* met then what Parsons calls 'regression' may occur, such as 'the "fall" of the western Roman Empire and the reversion of its territories to more or less "archaic" social conditions in the "dark ages"' (1966a: 4). Hence collapse takes place if ideology does not provide a legitimating 'cement' or if the economy is unable to provide the requisite goods and services in return for labour input. Parsons has made it amply clear that he sees social change as resulting 'from the operation of plural factors, all of which are mutually independent . . . *no* claim that social change is "determined" by economic interests, ideas, personalities of particular individuals, geographical conditions and so on, is acceptable. . . . Any factor is always interdependent with several others' (Parsons 1966a: 113). Hence for societies to reproduce themselves there must be reciprocity of exchange, in the long run, between the four functions described above.

A second complicating component of Parsons's model is the ordering of the functions of the system in 'a cybernetic sense'. Parsons uses the principle of a cybernetic hierarchy to help explain how the system is integrated and to explain change. In any system of action there is a hierarchical series of controls: at the apex of the hierarchy are units high in information, which *control* action; at the bottom of the hierarchy are units high in energy, which *condition* action. The overriding controlling function is performed by the pattern-maintenance (cultural values) subsystem, which at any given level of an action system controls the normative role structure (e.g. law), in turn the goal-attainment system (the polity) and then the adaptive sub-system (the economy) ($L\rightarrow I\rightarrow G \rightarrow A$). The cybernetic hierarchy determines the interaction of the system's parts, it governs order and change. The exchange of information and energy stimulate action.

But this paradigm as it stands is not satisfactory for our purposes. Devised against the background of American society, which has not experienced feudalism and capitalist revolution, it gives no central place to class conflict. Without development, it is unable to cope with the phenomenon of societal revolution. In my view, the interchange model accounts only for a special and ideal case at the societal level – it is an equilibrium analysis of (an idealised) American political system. This criticism has been made by Coser (1956: 21–4), Hacker (1961: 291) and Giddens (1968: 268). Such critics, however, do not suggest how Parsons's insights may be utilised and they throw out the baby with the bathwater.

The equal reciprocity of exchange is a special and not a universal case. To the cybernetic hierarchy of control must be added an analysis of the priority afforded in various social systems to different social functions and corresponding social groups. One of the weaknesses of the Parsonian model is that there is no adequate analysis of the source of values. Parsons would argue that values in a society are derived from the cultural system, but one needs also to understand that there are many values in the cultural system and that they are selected, interpreted and created by social groups. Rocher has put this another way when he claims that Parsons emphasises the role of 'controlling factors' (i.e. values) in determining action and that he underestimates the 'conditioning factors' – motivation for and constraints upon action. As Alexander has noted: 'The internal dimensions of values and norms ... have received vastly more of [Parsons's] attention than the conditional dimensions of economics and politics' (Alexander 1978: 192). Parsons exaggerated 'the dominance of values at the expense of other factors – material, psychological and social – on which individual and collective action depends' (Rocher 1974: 161).

This may be corrected by taking seriously Marxist theory which focusses on the level of productive forces and class interests. Hence in the analysis of the process of social change, *class* interests generate ideologies which legitimate different value systems, forms of politics, and types of adaptation. Marxism as a theoretical approach is useful and complementary because it makes central whose interests dominate in a social system: this gives them greater salience than just 'conditioning' factors. Rather than following Parsons by defining the subject matter of sociology as that of the 'integrative' function, I claim that Marxist analysis is more appropriate because it includes co-operation and conflict. Hence rather than focussing on what Parsons calls the 'societal community', I propose to redefine this as the class structure. Of course, 'integration' is an element of class analysis – for each ruling class seeks to legitimate its position, and for social co-operation to take place 'integration' must be achieved at certain levels: but societies in varying degrees also have disturbance and conflict. Hence the class structure (in a Marxist sense) must be given a central place in social analysis. Also the mode of production might for analytical purposes be considered as analogous to Parsons's stages of society.

Parsons, when studying a society, sees the economy as being a mechanism of 'adaptation', and the societal community as being concerned with patterns of 'integration'. I propose to allocate Marx's notion of the *level* of productive forces to the economy, A: this includes the 'adaptive' role of modern economics, but it includes much more besides. It postulates the conditioning role of technical forces of a mode of production. In Parsons's 'societal community' (I), I propose to include the *relations* to the means of production. This includes both class collaboration and class struggle. Parsons's stress on integration and the unitary nature of the societal community, I consider to be a special case. In Marxist terms, it defines the supremacy of a ruling class at the height of its power and with the absence of manifest class conflict predicated on antagonistic interests and ideologies. Apart from in an ideal communist society, the 'societal community' (I), to be realistic, must contain both integration and conflict: the balance between them is problematic. To 'socialisation' or pattern-maintenance and tension management (L) is attributed a complex of values including the reproduction of relations to the means of production and the values giving legitimacy to a system. To the 'polity' (G) are attributed the roles of administration and enforcement; Parsons's definition of the role of the polity as mobilisation of resources to attain designated ends fits quite well, if we bear in mind that it includes the use of force. 'The state' as such is not given a separate analytical place in my model: this is because modern Marxist analysis of the state has so widened its scope (to include repression, socialisation and ideology, e.g. Althusser 1971, Poulantzas 1973) that it has become an all-inclusive category and such activities are included under L, I and G. A diagram (Figure 3) contrasting Parsons's model and the suggested amendment is shown on page 119.

While Parsons in the tradition of liberal individualism underplays property and class systems, Marxists, at least until recently, have been equally one-sided. In the analysis of society, and of the impact of revolution in particular, they have been blind to aspects of society other than the class structure and the mode of production with their implications for alienation, consciousness and class rule. Parsonian analysis shifts the focus of attention away from zero-sum political conflict situations (such as class struggle) to consider culture and values, patterns of integration, politics as effective goal-attainment and economics as efficient utilisation of resources. Such analysis helps to locate revolutionary change not only in political revolution, but also in cultural, educational and economic revolutions.

THE CASE OF SOVIET RUSSIA

Let us attempt to apply Parsons's scheme to the analysis of the post-1917 period in Russia. In terms of the internal patterns of the new Soviet society these four inter-related sub-systems (discussed above) may be considered in order.

The patterns of values and beliefs of the Bolsheviks have been discussed in some detail and they may be considered to have formulated sets of goals for social action (L). They constitute not just an explanation of society but legitimate action for the rulers. It should also be clear that the actual cultural patterns of Soviet Russia were influenced by traditional values: these included not only values of Marxism but also feudal and bourgeois ones. The same may be said for the societal community, the polity and economy. In my analysis of Lenin's thought, I sought to bring out the importance of the indigenous Russian dimension to Lenin's ideas. The burden of my discussion of Mandel, Bettelheim, Tucker, Carr and Pethybridge was to show that the ideal 'supports' for building socialism did not exist. In the case of post-1917 Russia, for society to operate effectively on cultural values of socialism derived from classical Marxism there had to be a stock of 'socialist' personalities, a developed and dominant working class, an advanced political system and an appropriate economy to go with it. These Soviet Russia did not have. The interchanges between L, I, G and A were not reciprocated and did not 'balance' harmoniously.

Lenin provided a theoretical analysis of world capitalism which identified its essential political weakness in Russia, and he provided an acute political strategy for the seizure of political power; but more idealistic forms of 'socialism' were not sociologically possible in the Russian environment that the Bolsheviks inherited after 1917. The outcome was a complex form of adaptation between Bolshevism as a brand of Marxism and the traditional Russian environment. Lenin's version of Marxism was a primary ingredient to this social flux, but it was mediated by, and in turn changed by, other factors. The outcome

118

was not just a matter of 'becoming modern' on the model of the West, but included reversions to Tsarist forms of social organisation. As Tucker has noted, for instance, the bonding of individuals of all classes to state service is a continuity of the Tsarist system of *zakreposhchenie*; similarly, administrative exile and forced labour were reversions to pre-revolutionary practices.

PARSONS MODEL

L Socialisation   Societal community I
  (pattern-maintenance)

A Economy   Polity   G

AMENDED MODEL

L Socialisation   Class structure and I
  (production and   integrative system
   reproduction of the
   relations to the means
   of production)

A Economy   Polity   G
  (level of productive
   forces)

3. An amendment of Parsons's model of society

The analysis adopted by traditional Marxists emphasises the economic conditioning of a mode of production; other Marxists, particularly followers of Mao and other ultra-Leftists, in stressing *relationships* to the means of production, take a more voluntaristic approach, accentuating correct policy and leadership as major determinants in building socialism. The point of departure here is the relatively independent role played by culture and personality and the interconnexion between them and economy (level of productive forces) and polity.

What then are the implications of this approach for the study of the impact of the October Revolution? In Russia, Bolshevik theory was an amalgam of various values derived from the cultural system: these included not only Marxist ones but also those of a traditional Russian character. Ken Spours has noted the ways in which an integration of 'Marxism' and religion occurred in Stalin's Russia (1978:14). Where he errs, however, is in contrasting Bolshevism with 'trends in Russian political life' (p.13). Bolshevism was an expression of Russian Marxism which had absorbed much of the traditional Russian culture and differentiated it from Western European Marxism. This process did not begin after 1917 but was a continuation of an ongoing process. With the passage of time, Bolshevik values and beliefs intermeshed with the existing forms of integration, polity and economy: many Marxist ideals became replaced, or remained as ineffective rhetoric. The Civil War was fought and the New Economic Policy was devised because the integrative sub-system (the class structure) in Soviet Russia provided no general commitment to the values of the new rulers: the peasant masses were petty-bourgeois and had been socialised with the 'wrong values' – as far as building socialism was concerned. Hence we cannot generalise about the 'societal community' (I) simply in terms of 'integration'. Lenin's belief that the middle peasant would see that his long-term goals could only be met by some form of socialisation of the land proved too optimistic: the middle peasant remained committed to the exploitation of his own private plot of land. There were class interests here which created conflict. It has also been argued that both Lenin and Trotsky put their faith in the revolutionary consciousness of the masses in 1917 but, when confronted with the difficulties of reconstruction after 1917, they stressed the general 'backwardness' of the working class and their unpreparedness for socialism. (See, for instance, Knei-Paz 1978: 126–7.) There is a grain of truth here, but it is mistaken to chastise Lenin and Trotsky on this score, for both recognised that the level of consciousness of the masses which would respond to revolutionary leadership to *bring down* the autocracy and provisional government, was quite distinct from what was required to operate a true socialist system.

Two processes took place simultaneously: first, an attempt was made by the Bolshevik leadership to change the role structure of the integrative, political and economic sub-systems in line with their own version of their class interests given by their general theoretical orientation. The various sub-systems were isolated and 'inter-penetrated' by the state seeking to further a different system of exchanges. It is this (one-sided) process that theorists of totalitarianism have in mind. Second, the ongoing role structures feed back 'resistances' to these changes and modify them in line with practical possibilities. A process of osmosis takes place whereby orientations, practices and procedures socialised under the old regime are subject to change, but they also gradually modify the goals and beliefs of the leaders of the revolution. Study of this process shows that various institutional structures have some autonomy and may be able to 'resist' changes which take place in others, or at least be able to deflect them. Earlier, I mentioned Parsons's concept of a 'modal personality'. Lenin pointed out that the attitudes of the population were not conducive to the kinds of change that the Bolsheviks wanted to introduce. Parsons's discussion of personality is influenced by the American stratification system, but differentiation by status and sex is less important for this study. At the risk of oversimplifying, culturally the greatest social divide in Russia was that between town and country. The 'peasant mentality' which Lenin and Stalin had to contend with was largely 'hedonistic', seeking immediate gratification, whereas the leadership sought quite explicitly to impose more instrumental 'American' values. What did have ramifications throughout the whole social structure was the patriarchal and authoritarian nature of kinship relations, which was indicative of social relations in general. While the Bolsheviks also inherited many egalitarian and democratic values – from Western Marxist and Russian democratic thinkers – these were not widespread currency in Tsarist Russia; and equality did not figure much in Lenin's thought. Stalin's authoritarianism, and the acceptance of this authoritarianism, had its roots in the traditional system of values and personality. (Among the Bolsheviks, Lenin and Trotsky as well as Stalin were authoritarian, and even strident opponents of Stalin, such as Solzhenitsyn, exhibit similar characteristics, right down to the present day.) What I am suggesting is that (as Pomper has cogently summarised) 'value systems appropriate for modernisation emerge in relatively backward societies and ... new values and identities or personality structures issuing from the internalisation of new values and identities enter the modernising society by way of subcultures of rebellion. A new political leadership emerges imbued with the values of the subculture and nearing a new identity, and tries to remold the larger society in its own image' (Pomper 1978: 11). This in turn is conditioned by other traditional values and institutions.

Let us now move from culture to consider the social structure. The

Bolshevik Revolution of 1917 certainly brought about important changes in class relations. Formal rights to property and political power were severely and quickly altered and the foundations of the political order and the bases of the system of social stratification were transformed. But during the consolidation of power by the Bolsheviks different forms of social stratification persisted. (For education, see Lane 1973 but cf. McClelland 1978, Fitzpatrick 1978.) The cultural background of underprivileged strata to a considerable extent shapes their aspirations and expectations, thereby working against equality of opportunity. The creation of a 'new social consciousness' therefore may develop only partially (or not at all) in the class the revolution intended to benefit. The level of productive forces has a dominant effect on the occupational structure, on the kinds of jobs available, and it conditions the kinds of expectations that people have internalised. Changes in values which revolutionaries introduce at the societal level define, to quote Parsons, the kind of society which they think desirable (Parsons 1961: 79). But the institutionalisation of new values in the social system often meets with resistance. Previously formed class expectations remain. Occupational and status aspirations are both rooted deep in cultural traditions and limited by people's experience of production, and thus in order to change the 'definition of the meaning of the life of the individual in society' (*ibid.*: 78) the impact of revolution must be considered over generations.

This may be illustrated by consideration of the position of women. In education, the reason for the post-revolutionary improvement in the status of women lies in the fact that even before the Revolution urban females to a great extent had the same general cultural standards as the politically dominant males. When the legitimacy of the political domination of men was broken, no cultural brake prevented women from achieving equality in the sphere of education – though prejudice concerning women's occupation, of course, still remained. While women's educational and occupational status was significantly improved under Stalin, their position in the family and in power relationships with men hardly altered. This again I would explain by the relatively easier ways in which industrial jobs and places in higher education may be opened up by the political authorities – compared to what are, in effect, personal relations which are deeply embedded in cultural tradition. Traditional culture did not 'determine' the practices of Soviet society, and I am not advocating the case of cultural determinism in the sense used by Ruth Benedict; but the overriding values of Bolshevism were certainly 'conditioned' in many ways by cultural constraints. What has been wrongly identified as the 'introduction of socialism' in Soviet Russia under Stalin, must be interpreted as having an important *Russian* cultural component.

In the post-revolutionary period, what I have defined as the class and integration system acquires great importance. Not only does 'revolutionary law' try to destroy existing value commitments and impose different claims to loyalty, but penal sanctions, 'socialist' traditions and rituals are formulated which seek to promote identification with the new political values (see C. Lane 1981). These new sanctions, traditions and rituals, however, have to borrow extensively from the existing stock and indirectly continue pre-revolutionary practices: administrative exile, work in penal colonies and the cult of Lenin and Stalin – analogous to the supremacy of the Tsars – are examples here. One of the most puzzling attributes of Stalin's terror to many people is the loyalty of the population to him. This has been remarked on by writers quite hostile to Stalin, particularly by Medvedev who regards him as a criminal. It seems to me that Stalin did succeed in providing mechanisms of integration – diffuse sentiments of loyalty were given to the new regime. Gouldner dismisses this idea on the grounds that in an objective sense the 'interests of the system as a whole' were not being pursued (Gouldner 1978: 46). This, however, is an assumption based on a Parsonian and liberal notion that one can define the interests of a system as a whole, independently of class interests. He misses the point that not all interests can be pursued. Stalin's collectivisation campaign could be interpreted as an extension of Lenin's class analysis of the countryside. Lenin himself, in discussing the steps necessary to establish a socialist system, pointed out that 'Clearly, in order to abolish classes completely, it is not enough to overthrow the exploiters, the landowners and capitalists ... it is necessary to abolish *all* private ownership of the means of production. ... It is necessary to overcome the resistance (frequently passive which is particularly stubborn and particularly difficult to overcome) of the numerous survivals of small-scale production; it is necessary to overcome the enormous force of habit and conservatism which are connected with these survivals' (*A Great Beginning*, SW3: 174). Collectivisation may not have been the most efficient way of maintaining agricultural production: in the short run, it led to a decline in the head of livestock and to a fall in total grain production. But it was effective in the sense that it maintained political control and succeeded in increasing the supply of marketable grain (Ellman 1975; cf. Cohen 1977, who discusses Stalinism from the point of view of efficiency rather than effectiveness).

That Stalin's 'excesses' did unnecessarily weaken Soviet Russia is true, and it must be admitted that there was a pathological element in Stalin's make-up which led to hasty, senseless decision-making and to morally indefensible action. But that was not all. As Knei-Paz (1978: 436–7) has noted, there was a certain rationality about Stalin's rule, in the sense that his activities were related to achieving goals given by the Bolshevik Revolution – political control, industrialisation and modernisation. The political violence was at root a phenomenon caused by the lack of support in the country as a whole for Bolshevik policies and by the psychological state engendered by the world isolation of the Revolution. What appear to Western liberal-democrats as arbitrary, despotic (and illegitimate) forms of rule were not new to the Russian population; and had been taken for granted for centuries by the peasant masses. If Stalin's actions were morally indefensible, it seems to me to be difficult, if not impossible, to separate a critique of Stalin from a critique of Bolshevism.

The idea of a 'totalitarian' model of society as developed by the authors cited in Chapter 3 above, in my view, needs to be considerably modified. In the first place, as far as a traditional society is concerned, the segmentalisation of much of peasant life effectively precludes centralised political control. Secondly, political policies are socially and culturally conditioned: they have to take for granted the stock of personalities, the class structure and the traditional culture. These provide limits to the 'total control' of any politically dominant group seeking to enforce ideological goals on a social system. A modified version of a command system may be illustrated in the more neutral terms of my model. Such a system involves the domination of I (law enforcements and social control), fed by values coming from L (Marxist and traditional), these are aggregated through G (the polity) to raise the level of productive forces, A. (See Figure 4.) There would be very little feedback by G or A on L or I. This is the element of truth in the totalitarian model – the arrows pointing to A bring out the importance of economic development in Soviet Russia.

Turning to Parsons's societal interchange model described above

(Figure 2), we may illustrate how in practice Soviet Russia deviated from his model. Let us consider just the 'product' interchanges in more detail. In the A→G exchange, there was a relatively undeveloped 'commitment of services' to the collectivity, and very little reciprocated exchange with respect to G→A–money was not the medium of exchange for the allocation of fluid resources; direct administrative allocation replaced financial control. For L→A, again the role of money was irrelevant and rather than 'commodity exchange' having salience, both elements were replaced by an ideological value for capital accumulation. A→L: there was an undeveloped 'commitment' to production of goods and therefore very little exchange. I→G: 'political support' must be amended to include the use of coercion as well as idealistic compliance. G→I: leadership responsibility was little developed and had minimum exchange. L→I: 'value-based claims to loyalties' were strong and these were augmented by the charisma of Lenin, then of Stalin. I→L: 'commitments to common values' entailed in this case an exchange of traditional beliefs for Marxist–Leninist ones. A→I: 'grounds for justification of claims' did not originate in A and this exchange was poorly developed. I→A: ranking of claims in the sense of budgeting was replaced by ideological and administrative definition of priorities. G→L: under Stalin there was an absence of 'moral responsibility for collective interests', rather there was, if anything, a recognition by the leadership of the necessity of action. L→G: 'legality of powers of office' this did not exist in a formal Western sense, rather the need for decisive action was a legitimation of the use of force.

The Revolution carried out a complete change in the relations of man to property. State ownership of the means of production, presided over by the Communist Party, ensured the socialist nature of class relations in a formal ownership sense. This has secured a different type of production to that known under capitalism, which is not a temporary phenomenon but has been institutionalised into recurring sets of relationships. It involves central economic planning by the government, commodity production and exchange. But there is an absence of a capital market and there is no extraction of surplus through market relations which accrues to a ruling class. The level of productive forces, however, is not sufficient to support a socialist superstructure and therefore the state's activity is directed to *create* socialist social relations (the new 'communist man'). The Revolution was one 'from above', not from below. The superstructure includes elements drawn from other modes of production, particularly a bourgeois form of distribution of commodities and a traditional culture. For both Marxist and Parsonian analysis, development of the level of production forces is crucial for societal advancement. Without the Bolshevik Revolution, Russia could well have stagnated (like Poland at that time) or disintegrated – like Zaire or Rhodesia in the 1970s.

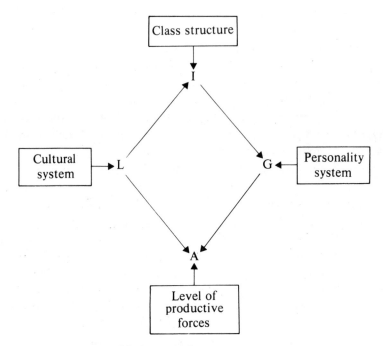

4. Modified command system
   Boxes illustrate systems external to society.

The notion of revolution, therefore, must be understood as including different rates of change: in the polity, a government and a ruling group may be replaced quickly, but the implementation of social and cultural revolutionary goals, such as equality of educational opportunity, is often a protracted affair. Revolution then should be conceived of as a process including a transitional period in which new institutions embodying the values of the revolution are introduced but coexist with the old values persisting from the *ancien régime*, and thus forms of incompatibility continue into what is called the 'post-revolutionary' epoch.

Revolution is not necessarily ineffective as an instrument of social change if the ultimate values of the revolutionaries are not immediately translated into effective policies: 'conditioning' factors here are crucial. After 1917 in Russia, Marxism–Leninism was not institutionalised into a normative ideology providing an internalised belief system: after the resolution of the political part of the revolutionary struggle during the Civil War, the value system of Marxism–Leninism was utilised to legitimate Stalin's dominant role; it reflected the elite's political interests in maintaining power as much as the 'original' values of Marx and Lenin. While it is true that Marxism–Leninism remained a set of values, or long-term goals, it also became a legitimating ideology. Principles are turned into practice in the light of objective possibility. As Parsons had pointed out, in the Soviet Union under Stalin occurred the 're-equilibration of society' (1951: 529): the need for adaptive structures (e.g. differential rewards) was recognised and the family became a recognised institution for social stability and individual integration. In other words, the conditioning roles of sub-systems 'feed back' on the legitimating value system of Marxism–Leninism and modify it. The stark but modified model of a command system, described above, began to adopt more of the 'exchanges' of the Parsonian paradigm described in Figures 1 and 2.

Hence the explanation I am suggesting is a multi-relational one, rather than something to be found in the personal power of Stalin, or the reversal to 'state capitalism'. Armed uprising and armed force established the primacy of the Party and the political apparatus, their legitimacy was based on Marxist assumptions. But the groups which controlled the various apparatuses were powerful enough to 'feed back' their 'energy' onto the controlling ideology. This is the process aptly described by Weber as elective affinity (Gerth and Mills: 62–3). By examining *whose* values have primacy in a society we are able to distinguish ruling elites and classes and major cleavages in the society. The 'logic of development' under socialism may be limited by the structural constraints we have considered, but it does not follow from this that there is no choice, that there is only *one* correct policy for all countries. The different trajectories of development followed by various socialist countries leads us to beware of this methodological trap. By recognising the 'energy' of the political system one is able to formulate a separate paradigm of a society undergoing directed change. Such an approach to Soviet society has the advantage that it takes account of historically determined ethno-national cultural factors and their intermeshing with Marxist values.

Let me summarise some of the implications of this approach for the analysis of the revolutionary process. First, the character of the society before the processes of socialist revolution and industrialisation has made a considerable difference to the kind of regime that the communist political elites have been able to introduce. A second implication is that only institutional forces able to utilise considerable 'energy' can carry through large-scale social changes in bureaucratic empires such as Tsarist Russia. Under Bolshevik leadership, centralisation of political control and a strong bureaucratic state, inherited from pre-revolutionary Russia, ensured the introduction of capital development on a large scale. The other side of this coin has been the absence of wider forms of real participation and control by the public at large: in a Parsonian sense there has been little consumer choice in the economy or polity. Finally, a third objective of this approach is to point to the structural limitations of revolution. Men do not make their history as they please, but under constraints given by the level of productive forces, by the 'stocks' of personality with given class orientations and the cultural conditions they inherit. Many explanations of the 'degeneration' of the Soviet Union emphasise 'external' constraints – the hostile capitalist world framework. These factors are no doubt important, but much more emphasis must be placed on other conditioning factors if the impact and course of revolutionary seizures of power are to be understood.

The Russian Revolution was a process which continued under Stalin. Lenin provided the general strategy for *political* change, for bringing about fundamental alterations in man's ownership relations to property; and this does not fit easily into social system analysis as developed by Parsons. Here Lenin's analysis of the uneven development of capitalism, the hegemonic role of the Party through the dictatorship of the proletariat, led to events which began the revolutionary process in Russia. Under Stalin, the economic process of adaptive upgrading – developing the level of productive forces – was achieved. Class relations included civil strife and not only did Stalin become a charismatic leader, which ensured a high level of loyalty, but he resorted to penal sanctions and the use of terror against opponents.

These methods were sometimes irrational and were often immoral, but in sum they contributed to societal integration. Value generalisation – the ideology of Soviet Marxism–Leninism, influenced by traditional values – provided legitimation to the whole process.

ʋʋʋ

Epilogue:
different routes to socialism?

The foregoing discussion has put Lenin's thought, his prognostications for revolution, into a cultural context. I have argued that Lenin's theories, tactics and methods were apposite to Russia of the early twentieth century and that they have an affinity with many countries today which are at a low level of economic development and dominated economically by a capitalist metropolis. Lenin's genius as a Marxist thinker was to turn Marxism from being an analysis of Europe to being one of Asia: Leninism has become an ethic of development, of industrialisation, rather than a critique of contemporary capitalist society. Stalin's rule, cruel and tyrannical though it was, was a Marxist form of development and was a continuation of the Russian Revolution. In this perspective, Europe of the 1980s faces different problems and possesses a quite contrasting intellectual, political, economic and social structure which makes much of Lenin's analysis inappropriate today; and Stalin's objectives and methods are irrelevant. But Marxism as a movement of social criticism has to some extent been imprisoned by its Leninist past, and there has been a reaction against the degeneration of Marxism in the USSR under Stalin, and despair at the failure of Western Marxism to overthrow capitalism. Symbolically, Kolakowski's volume entitled *The Breakdown of Marxism* opens with a chapter on 'The Beginnings of Stalinism' (Kolakowski 1978: vol. 3). Anderson has shrewdly concluded that one of the 'fundamental emblems' of Western Marxist thought since the 1920s has been its 'common and latent *pessimism* . . . method as impotence, art as consolation, pessimism as quiescence' (Anderson 1976: 88,94). Following Lenin's death in 1924, a gloomy evaluation of the Soviet Union was paralleled by the rejection of its ideological conditioning forces – Marxism–Leninism. But these reactions against Leninism have generated little in the form of an alternative Marxist dynamic. As Anderson has pointed out: 'The concentration of theorists into professional philosophy, together with the discovery of Marx's own early writings, led to a general retrospective search for intellectual ancestries to Marxism in anterior European philosophical thought and a reinterpretation of historical materialism in the light of them' (Anderson 1976: 93). This is a somewhat harsh and unfair judgement on contemporary Marxism, as it overlooks the valuable contribution of such writers as Althusser, Poulantzas and Habermas. (See Herf 1977: 139–40.) It also ignores the political activity of Western Marxist revolutionary groups (e.g. The Communist Party, Workers Revolutionary Party) directly involved with the working class. My intention here has been to show how Marxism–Leninism, as it has developed in the USSR, has been a policy useful for Russian conditions but inappropriate in the West.

Lenin drew much of his intellectual inspiration from Russian revolutionary thinkers concerned with the problem of serfdom and the rise of capitalism. In contemporary Europe, there is no 'peasant question' analogous to that facing early twentieth-century Russia, and such topics as underground revolutionary activity, though of interest for comparative purposes, are not a major concern. The dominant political movement and culture among both the working class and intellectuals, at least in Britain, is social-democracy. Social-democracy is a hybrid doctrine and movement: it contains elements drawn from Marxism, utopian socialism, Christianity and liberal-bourgeois democracy; the movement includes revolutionary, reformist and capitalist apologetic elements. Its cultural heritage, including that of the communists, is steeped in liberal ideas and democratic ideology. Compared with pre- or postrevolutionary Russia, the political culture is more diverse, more open and, despite many forms of repression, more democratic: human rights have been secured, if not fully practised. Parliaments, trade unions and workers' parties are well established: none was so in Lenin's Russia. The ideology of the masses is secular and ingrained with bourgeois culture: it is a world apart from the peasant masses of 1917. The intellectual· leadership of the working class is largely reformist, seeking improvements within the parameters of capitalism; in Russia, and in many developing countries today, the indigenous leaders were foremost revolutionaries (not necessarily Marxists) seeking to overthrow autocratic and feudal regimes. The ideology of revolutionary Marxism, therefore, must in some ways come to grips with quite a new cultural situation. It must address itself to the fact that literacy is universal, that

131

the leaders and members of the working class wish to capitalise as consumers on the advances given by capitalism of a bourgeois-democratic variety. The structures of social integration go much deeper, are more subtle and more comprehensive than in the time of Marx and Lenin. The twentieth-century revolutions in communications and in education ensure the continued exposure of the masses and their leaders to the inculcation of a constantly changing barrage of indoctrination to the system, and various 'within system' forms of criticisms of it.

The massive oppression of the labouring masses of the nineteenth and early twentieth centuries – the absence of rights of combination, the grinding poverty, the lack of provision for the unemployed, the sick and needy – has been superseded, or, at least, greatly alleviated. Lenin's description of social relations under feudalism and capitalism may be clearly located in pre-revolutionary Russia and are a caricature of the West in the 1980s. 'The feudal organisation of social labour rested on the discipline of the bludgeon, while the working people, robbed and tyrannised by a handful of landowners, were utterly ignorant and downtrodden. The capitalist organisation of social labour rested on the discipline of hunger, and, notwithstanding all the progress of bourgeois culture and bourgeois democracy, the vast mass of the working people in the most advanced, civilised and democratic republics remained an ignorant and downtrodden mass of wage-slaves or oppressed peasants, robbed and tyrannised by a handful of capitalists' (Lenin, *A Great Beginning*, SW 3: 173). Integration, in the sense of a communality of values and beliefs, is now greater than in earlier times: it rests on strong, politically aware unions and well-organised mass workers' parties, on comprehensive social services providing minimum standards in times of adversity. Politics has become minority* group politics (women, Blacks) or economistic (the struggle for income or jobs), or redistributive (tax, education, welfare) rather than class politics. The level of class consciousness in a Marxist sense is low. Trade unions play an important role in mediating between worker and state apparatus and employer. Their role is not only manifestly expressive but, unintentionally perhaps, unions are a cementing flux in the social structure. They provide regularised and institutional means of the expression and control of the interests of the working class. There is a high level of social·integration. A dominant right-wing social-democracy (the liberals and apologetic petty bourgeoisie) represents a

---

* 'minority' in the sense of a sub-group within a larger group bound by some special ties, *not* in a demographic numerical sense.

stronger shell for capitalism than does Lenin's characterisation of Parliamentary democracy.

Lenin advocated the dictatorship of the proletariat following a socialist revolution: to argue otherwise would be to destroy one of the central pillars of Lenin's world view. The major question, as I would pose it, is not whether the dictatorship of the proletariat is central to Lenin's thought (there is no doubt that it is – see Slaughter 1978), but how appropriate his recommendations now are for Western Europe. Looked at in the perspective of early twentieth-century Russia, the term takes on a different connotation than it does today. The Bolsheviks after 1917 had to carry out a revolution from above, in a country with a peasantry which, once its rights to land were assured, was hostile to socialism: there was a low level of social integration. They were a modernising party as much as a socialist party. In Western Europe, the appeals of such modernisation have no political resonance: 'electrification of the countryside' appears as an historical fossil. Similarly, the widespread repressive activity of the Soviet state, particularly under Stalin, would no longer serve the same kinds of political ends. The mass of the population in advanced capitalist states would lose nothing by the state ownership and control of the means of production. The rise of the joint stock company and the growing institutionalisation of ownership have depersonalised the business bourgeoisie and have placed the affairs of business firms in the hands of salaried managers: they objectively have little to lose, and possibly something to gain, by public ownership. While it is true that the working class as an ascendant class does not create its own 'socialist' mode of production under capitalism (as did the bourgeoisie under feudalism), the working class nevertheless is in possession of the workings of capital, as the joint stock company has effectively separated owners from the process of production. The elimination of private business through public ownership in the era of the large corporation, and the replacement of the capital market by planning would not promote such massive unrest as in Russia which had a large petty-bourgeois peasantry. Hence changes in ownership relations and the supersession of the capitalist mode of production could be achieved without a head-on clash between bourgeoisie and working class, analogous to that between feudal landowner and bourgeoisie.

The notion of 'the proletariat' now conjures up a picture not congruent with that of the modern working class. In Lenin's day, in the rapidly developing industries of Russia, the skilled manual worker in the metal-working industries and in mining and transport constituted the core of the working class. Today, the 'working class' is much more heterogeneous in its occupational composition. The extractive and productive industries are declining at the expense of the tertiary sector. The white-coated worker, the salesman, the scientist/technologist, the teacher, local and national government officials (including health and social workers) have increased in number and form part of a working class in which the social homogeneity of the traditional toiler (if it ever existed) has been replaced by a privatised and instrumental life-style. The social vision of such strata does not include the polarised class conflict images of society characterising the Russian proletariat and peasantry. In the last analysis, force may be necessary to maintain the working class in power: but it is unlikely to be analogous to the Red Guards of October 1917, or the penal colonies of Stalin's Russia. The state has to be conceived of as being composed of those institutions and groups that reproduce capitalist relations to the means of production: the antagonistic collision between the police and the revolutionary no longer symbolises the form of control and conflict, which is now manipulative in form and widespread in scope to include the mass media and the formal educational system. At the same time, the advanced economies of the West suffer regular periods of decline, and the probability of long-term economic advance is now an optimistic standpoint. The state has to contain structural imbalances, deindustrialisation and its ensuing problems of unemployment.

As to politics, Lenin's Party was not only an instrument of struggle for the attainment of revolutionary goals, but it became a major power in the administration of things and in the direction of affairs after 1917. Such a Party was in a unique position: it was born in the underground in a context of the working class (widely defined) being in an unorganised relatively masslike state. It was able to articulate a working-class interest and was able to impose this over the other weakly organised groupings: unlike in the West, the party of the working class preceded the tradeunionisation of that class. Under the circumstances of 1917, there was no other way that the class interest of workers could be articulated but through the Party. When in power, the Party could not rely on widespread support or on cadres of workers sufficiently educated to become more or less autonomous levers of policy-making and enforcement. The new incumbents of power lacked the personnel to put a socialist revolution into practice. They had to be taught. Administration became centralised, not only because it was so under the Tsars, but because the new administrators had insufficient skills. The Party had to become the 'leader, teacher, friend'; it had to tell people what to do. In the 1980s in the West, such a concept is no longer appropriate. The cultural level of the population is qualitatively different to what it was in Russia in Lenin's and Stalin's time. Direct participation in the management of things, in the ordering of priorities, is now much more feasible. 'Workers' control' need not be limited to a kind of political oversight of the captains of industry but, along with various forms of 'consumer' participation in administration, may be the expression of people's needs. Systemic change may only occur through a social movement accepted by a wide range of social strata composing the working class (broadly defined). Lenin's type of Party with a kernel of conscious revolutionary Marxists did provide such 'energy' (to use Parsons's term) in Russia: both to carry out the October coup and to enforce revolutionary gains under Lenin. In the 1980s, however, it is no longer apposite as a lever of revolution in advanced capitalist countries. A revolutionary political party now needs to be more of an aggregate of trade unions and local socialist groups and radical organisations, rather than the provider of centralised thinking for the masses. This, of course, does not mean that leadership is not of great importance: leadership now requires an analysis of inter-strata alliances (blue and white collar) and an aggregation of interests similar to Lenin's *smychka* with the peasantry, but completely different in form. Leadership should not only provide an alternative to capitalism, but must show how its promises can be fulfilled. This is the challenge to hybrid social-democracy: for its leaders to produce a policy for the replacement of capitalism (through genuine reform) which will be resonant to the structural imbalances of capitalism and which will appeal to a wide range of social strata.

Lenin himself did not see even the pre-revolutionary Bolshevik Party as having a narrow social or political focus: at the forefront of this thinking was the notion that the party should generalise a Marxist policy on the basis of a wide range of social grievances and conflicts. In contemporary Western Europe no Marxist Party can come to power independently of the mass trade-union movement, or of the organised forces of labour in social-democratic parties; and to be effective it must have the support of many middle-strata technical and supervisory staff. These groups are the political expression of the working class. Similarly, in terms of management of the economy, the problem is not one of development, of creating the bases of socialism as it has been in Soviet Russia, but of allowing a myriad exchanges between various sectors and interests rather in the way conceptualised by Parsons (see Figure 2 above). Indeed, as I have argued elsewhere, Parsons, properly interpreted, is a theorist laying bare the conditions for communism, not capitalism (Lane 1978).

Finally, we must consider the level of productive forces and the process of adaptation. Lenin's greatest political achievement was to perceive that countries undergoing capitalist development under conditions of traditional autocracies and lacking an indigenous capitalist class, were ripe for a socialist revolution, in the sense of the abolition of private ownership of the means of production. It need hardly be repeated that Russia, and nearly all countries which have followed the same road, had a level of productive forces akin to the *beginning* of a capitalist mode of production. The theory of imperialism legitimated a socialist revolution, in Marxist terms, in underdeveloped countries, but Lenin also believed that there would be 'feedback' effects on the stability of the advanced countries. The closing up of foreign markets, the relative economic decline of the West and the economic crises there created by the OPEC countries have led to political instability: Lenin's prognosis in *Imperialism* is not without validity. But the advanced capitalist countries, though rapacious in policy to the Third World, have become relatively more self-sufficient and more independent in terms of trade. They have outstripped their levels of productive capacity of the early twentieth century. The technology at the disposal of man is capable of the production of even greater wealth. The problem is now one of utilising such resources for the public good: of maintaining production in the face of uncertainties of demand, of maintaining employment, of harnessing science to exploit the adaptive capacity of nature, of providing conditions for the labour force to work continuously and efficiently. The problem of adaptation is now one of politics, not of economics (in the sense of overcoming scarcity). In advanced countries (despite grave maldistribution of resources) the problems of supply of facilities to meet human needs, to alleviate poverty, have been mainly solved. A socialist movement must reorient itself to addressing the problems of providing more meaningful work, of the better use of resources, of ensuring political conditions for collective action.

Marxists following in the steps of Lenin have for long focussed on the collapse of social 'integration' in modern capitalist societies: they have interpreted collapse in terms of social disintegration, of polarised social relations between the two major classes of bourgeoisie and proletariat. Popular social consciousness, however, seems to be increasingly 'integrative': this is reflected in workers' movements becoming increasingly revisionistic. In my view, the focus of attention should be shifted to problems of *system* integration. Collapse is more likely to occur because of contradictions between various parts of the social system and with the network of reciprocated exchanges necessary for social equilibrium not being maintained. The potential of the system, given by the objective level of the productive forces (the economy) is not fulfilled by the class system. In Parsonian terms, there is lack of reciprocity *between* I and A. (See above p. 112.) This is at root a contradiction between the level of productive forces and the class system. Also the polity is under strain to make arrangements for the effective allocation of resources (the G–A exchange): it is faced with price inflation, with unemployment of capital (underproduction) and of labour (unemployment), with increasing difficulties presented by organised labour, which does not accept the terms of employment, of the returns from work (the A–L exchange). These are not ephemeral but structural problems of capitalism. Hence, rather than collapse in terms of a lack of social integration, of polarised class consciousness (within I), it is more likely to occur through system distintegration – the incapacity of government and economy to fulfil expectations given by the value system and beliefs internalised through socialisation. These are structural manifestations of the class system: in the sense of ownership relations and the reproduction of such relations. The situation preceding the February Revolution of 1917 in Russia may be more analogous to contemporary Western Europe than that of October and the ensuing Civil War. The autocracy collapsed: there was no objective need for a 'dictatorship of the bourgeoisie'.

These are problems which go outside Lenin's conception of socialist revolution. They are foreign to the symbolism of ultra-leftist concepts of hegemonic Party, armed insurrection, violent street fighting and bitter class struggle – class struggle now has a much wider and sophisticated form. Rather than ploughing over Lenin's work for insight into what he 'really' said, and trying to legitimate political activity in terms of Lenin's political genius, the message of this book is that Lenin's substantive politics and their continuation by J. Stalin are appropriate for different sets of problems to those that confront Europe in the last quarter of the twentieth century. Lenin saw that Marx's solutions were being dogmatically applied to problems of capitalism in early twentieth century Russia. Lenin's *approach* was a development of Marxism. One must not make the same mistakes as Lenin's opponents over Marx and attempt to apply Lenin's solutions (the content of Lenin's thought) to societies which have changed out of all recognition from the ones that he analysed. Rather than: 'Lenin lived, Lenin lives, Lenin shall live' (Maya-kovski), our motto should be: 'Lenin was a man, he lived and died.' But the tendency of Western Marxism – as outlined by Anderson – to intro-version, to divorce from political practice, to philosophising about the world, to concern with culture, is also unlikely to lead to significant social change. The alternative is greater participation in the mass move-ments of the working class – particularly the trade unions and social-democratic parties – and the politicisation and provision of leadership for these movements. One vital lesson to be learned from Lenin for con-temporary Marxism is the importance of political practice.

References

wwwwwwwwwwwwwwwwwwwwwwwwwwwwwwwwwwwwwwwwwwwwwwwwwwwwwwwwwwwwwwwwwwwwwwwwwwwwwwww

Adler, A., Cohen, F., Decaillot, M., Frioux, C. and Robel, L. (1978). *L'URSS et nous*, Paris: Editions Sociales.

Alexander, J. C. (1978). 'Formal and Substantive Voluntarism in the work of Talcott Parsons: A Theoretical and Ideological Reinterpretation', *American Sociological Review*, vol. 43.

Althusser, L. (1971). *Lenin and Philosophy and Other Essays*, London: New Left Books.

Althusser, L. (1975). *Essays in Self-Criticism*, London: New Left Books.

Althusser, L. and Balibar, E. (1970). *Reading Capital*, London: New Left Books.

Anderson, P. (1976). *Considerations on Western Marxism*, London: New Left Books.

Atkinson, D. (1972). *Orthodox Consensus and Radical Alternative*, London: Heinemann.

Avineri, S. (1968). *The Social and Political Thought of Karl Marx*, Cambridge: Cambridge University Press.

Balibar, E. (1977). *On the Dictatorship of the Proletariat*, London: New Left Books.

Barfield, R. (1971). 'Lenin's Utopianism: State and Revolution', *Slavic Review*, vol. 30, no. 1.

Baron, S. H. (1963). *Plekhanov: The Father of Russian Marxism*, London: Routledge.

Bellis, P. (1979). *Marxism and the USSR*, London: Macmillan.

Berdyaev, N. (1937). *The Origin of Russian Communism*, London: Geoffrey Bles.

Bettelheim, C. (1972). 'On the Transition to Socialism', in P. M. Sweezy and C. Bettelheim (eds.), *On the Transition to Socialism*, New York: Monthly Review Press.

Bettelheim C. (1975). *The Transition to Socialist Economy*, London: Harvester Press.

Bettelheim, C. (1977). *Class Struggles in the USSR: First Period 1917–1923*, Sussex: Harvester Press.

Blain, R. A. (1971). 'An Alternative to Parsons' Four-Function Paradigm as a Basis for Developing General Sociological Theory', in *American Sociological Review*, vol. 35, no. 4.

Blondel, J. (1969). *Comparative Government: a Reader*, London: Macmillan.

Bochenski, J. M. (1962). 'Three Components of Communist Ideology', in *Studies in Soviet Thought*, vol. 2.

139

References

Bochenski, J. M. (1963). *Soviet Russian Dialectical Materialism*, Dordrecht.

Bottomore, T. (1975). *Marxist Sociology*, London: Macmillan.

Brym, R. J. (1978). *The Jewish Intelligentsia and Russian Marxism*, London: Macmillan.

Buick, A. (1975). 'The Myth of the Transitional Society', in *Critique*, no. 5.

Carew-Hunt, R. N. (1963). *The Theory and Practice of Communism*, Harmondsworth: Penguin.

Carr, E. H. (1958). *Socialism in One Country*, vol.1, London: Macmillan.

Carr, E. H. (1966). *A History of Soviet Russia. The Bolshevik Revolution 1917–1923*, Harmondsworth: Penguin. (Vol.1, first published by Macmillan, 1950; vol.3, first published by Macmillan, 1953.)

Carrillo, S. (1977). *'Eurocommunism' and the State*, London: Lawrence and Wishart.

Claudin-Urondo, C. (1977). *Lenin and the Cultural Revolution*, Sussex: Harvester Press.

Cohen, G. A. (1978). *Karl Marx's Theory of History: a Defence*, London: Oxford University Press.

Cohen, S. F. (1977). 'Bolshevism and Stalinism', in R. C. Tucker, *Stalinism*, New York: Norton.

Conquest, R. (1972). *Lenin*, London: Fontana.

Corrigan, P. and Leonard, P. (1978). *Social Work Practice under Capitalism: A Marxist Approach*, London: Macmillan.

Corrigan, P., Ramsay, H. R. and Sayer, D. (1978). *Socialist Construction and Marxist Theory: Bolshevism and its Critique*, London: Macmillan.

Corrigan, P., Ramsay, H. R. and Sayer, D. (1979). 'The Historical Experience of Bolshevism', paper given at the New School of Social Research, New York.

Coser, L. A. (1956). *The Functions of Social Conflict*, Glencoe, Ill.: The Free Press.

Daniels, R. (1953). 'The State and Revolution', in *American Slavonic and East European Review*, vol. 21.

Davies, R. W. (1979). 'Ruthless Dictator or Prisoner of Coercion?', in *Times Higher Education Supplement*, 21 December.

Deutscher, I. (1954). *The Prophet Armed*, London: Oxford University Press.

Dunn, J. (1972). *Modern Revolutions*, Cambridge: Cambridge University Press.

Eldridge, J. E. T. (1971). *Max Weber*, London: Nelson.

Ellman, M. (1975). 'Did the Agricultural Surplus Provide the Resources for the Increase in Investment in the USSR during the First Five Year Plan?', in *Economic Journal*, vol. 85.

Engels, F., 'Karl Marx, *A Contribution to the Critique of Political Economy*', in Marx and Engels (1958), *SW* 1: 366–76.

Engels, F., 'Prefatory Note to *The Peasant War in Germany*', in Marx and Engels (1958), *SW* 1: 640–56.

Engels, F., 'Ludwig Feuerbach and the End of Classical German Philosophy', in Marx and Engels (1951), *SW* 2: 324–67.

Fairs, K.M. (1974). *'Alliance': The Relationship between the Theory of Alliance and the Practical Policy of Alliance as Implemented in Russia in the Period 1918–1927*, M.Sc. (Econ), University of Wales.

Fitzpatrick, S. (ed.) (1978). *Cultural Revolution in Russia, 1928–1931*, Blooming-

References

ton: Indiana U.P.

Fleron, F.J. Jr. (1977a). 'The Western Connection: Technical Rationality and Soviet Politics', in *Soviet Union*, vol.4, no.1.

Fleron, F.J. Jr. (1977b). 'For the Sixtieth Anniversary of the October Revolution', in *Labour Review*, vol.1, no.5.

Franklin, B. (ed.). (1973). *The Essential Stalin*, London: Croom Helm.

Friedgut, T.H. (1979). *Political Participation in the USSR*, Princeton, New Jersey: Princeton University Press.

Garaudy, R. (1970). *The Turning-Point of Socialism*, London: Collins.

Geras, N. (1977). 'Lenin, Trotsky and the Party', in *International*, vol.4, no.2.

Gerratana, V. (1977). 'Stalin, Lenin and "Leninism"', in *New Left Review*, no. 103.

Gerth, H.H. and Mills, C.W. (1948). *From Max Weber*, London: Routledge and Kegan Paul.

Giddens, A. (1968). '"Power" in the Recent Writings of Talcott Parsons', in *Sociology*, vol.2, no.3.

Ginsburg, N. (1979). *Class, Capital and Social Policy*, London: Macmillan.

Gottschalk, L. (1944). 'Cause of Revolution', in *American Journal of Sociology*, vol.50, no.1.

Gouldner, A.W. (1959). 'Reciprocity and Autonomy in Functional Theory', in Llewellyn Gross (ed.), *Symposium on Sociological Theory*, New York: Harper.

Gouldner, A.W. (1971). *The Coming Crisis of Western Sociology*, London: Heinemann.

Gouldner, A.W. (1978). 'Stalinism: A Study of Internal Colonialism', in *Telos*, no.34.

Gurr, R.C. (1973). 'The Revolution—Social-Change Nexus', in *Comparative Politics*, vol.5, no.3.

Gurr, T.R. (1970). *Why Men Rebel*, Princeton, New Jersey: Princeton University Press.

Hacker, A. (1961). 'Sociology and Ideology', in Max Black, *The Social Theories of Talcott Parsons*, Englewood Cliffs; N.J.: Prentice-Hall.

Haimson, L. (1955). *The Russian Marxists and the Origins of Bolshevism*, Cambridge, Mass.: Harvard University Press.

Hammond, T.T. (1957). *Lenin on Trade Unions and Revolution 1893–1917*, New York: Columbia University Press. (Republished by Greenwood Press, 1974.)

Harding, N. (1975). 'Lenin's Early Writings—The Problem of Context', in *Political Studies*, vol.23, no.4.

Harding, N. (1977). *Lenin's Political Thought*, vol.1: Theory and Practice in the Democratic Revolution.

Harding, N. (1980). *Lenin's Political Thought*, vol.2: Theory and Practice in the Socialist Revolution, London: Macmillan. (In press)

Herf, J. (1977). 'Science and Class or Philosophy and Revolution: Perry Anderson on Western Marxism', in *Socialist Revolution*, vol.7, no.35

Hindess, B. and Hirst, P. (1977). *Mode of Production and Social Formation*, London: Macmillan.

Hobsbawm, E. (1973). 'Lenin and the "Aristocracy of Labour"', in E. Hobsbawm (ed.), *Revolutionaries*, London: Weidenfeld & Nicolson.

References

Hoffman, J. (1975). *Marxism and the Theory of Praxis*, London: Lawrence and Wishart.

Horowitz, I.V. 'Socialism and the Problem of Knowledge' in Parekh (1975).

Hyman, R. (1971). *Marxism and the Sociology of Trade Unionism*, London: Pluto.

Inkeles, A. (1966). 'Models in the Analysis of Soviet Society, in *Survey*, no.60.

Johnson, C. (ed.) (1970). *Change in Communist Systems*, Stanford: Stanford Universities Press.

Johnstone, M. (1967). 'Marx and Engels and the Concept of the Party', in R. Miliband and J. Saville (eds.), *The Socialist Register 1967*, London: Merlin.

Johnstone, M. (1970). 'Socialism, Democracy and the One-Party System', in *Marxism Today*, vol.14.

Karpovich, M. (1944). 'A Forerunner to Lenin: P.N. Tkachev', in *Review of Politics*, vol.6.

Keat, R. and Urry, J. (1975). *Social Theory as Science*, London: Routledge.

Kelle, V.Zh. *et al.* (1970). *Leninizm i dialektika obshchestvennogo razvitiya*, Moscow.

Kemp, T. (1967). *Theories of Imperialism*, London: Dobson.

Kemp-Welch, A. (1978). 'Stalinism and Intellectual Order', unpublished discussion paper, St Antony's College, Oxford.

Kilroy-Silk, R. (1972). *Socialism Since Marx*, London: Allen Lane.

Knei-Paz, B. (1978). *The Social and Political Thought of Leon Trotsky*, Oxford: Clarendon Press.

Kolakowski, L. (1978). *Main Currents of Marxism*, 3 vols., London: Oxford University Press.

Kolakowski, L. and Hampshire, S. (1974). *The Socialist Idea*, London: Weidenfeld and Nicolson.

Korsch, K. (1970). *Marxism and Philosophy*, London: New Left Books.

Korsch, K. (1972). *Three Essays on Marxism*, New York: Monthly Review Press.

Korsch, K. (1975). 'Lenin's Philosophy', in A. Pannekoek, *Lenin as Philosopher*, London: Merlin. (Note. This essay is incorrectly attributed to Paul Mattick in some copies of this edition.)

K.P.S.S. (1953). *KPSS v rezolyutsiyakh i resheniyakh s'ezdov konferentsiy i plenumov Ts K*, Moscow: Gospolitizdat.

Krushchev, N. S. (1977). *Krushchev Remembers*, 2 vols. Harmondsworth: Penguin.

Lane, C. (1981). *The Rites of Rulers*. Cambridge: Cambridge University Press.

Lane, D. (1973). 'The Impact of Revolution on the Selection of Students for Higher Education: Soviet Russia, 1917–1928', in *Sociology*, vol. 7.

Lane, D. (1974). 'Leninism as an ideology of Soviet Development', in E. de Kadt and G. Williams (eds.), *Sociology and Development*, London: Tavistock.

Lane, D. (1975). *The Roots of Russian Communism*, London: Martin Robertson.

Lane, D. (1978). 'Towards a Political Sociology of State Socialist Society', in S. McInnes, I. W. McGrath and P. J. Potichnyj, *The Soviet Union and East Europe into the 1980s*, Ontario: Mosaic.

Lenin, V. I. *Selected Works*, in 3 vols. (Moscow: 1977 edition).

    SW   1:Karl Marx   pp. 15–43

           The Three Sources and Three Component Parts of Marxism   44–8

References

	What is to be Done?	92–241
	Two Tactics of Social-Democracy in the Democratic Revolution	425–527
SW	2:The Tasks of the Proletariat in the Present Revolution	pp. 29–35
	The Impending Catastrophy and How to Combat it	182–218
	The State and Revolution	238–327
	How to Organise Competition	457–74
SW	3:A Great Beginning	pp. 160–3
	'Left-Wing' Communism – An Infantile Disorder	291–370
	Better Fewer, but Better	829–42

Lenin, V. I. *Collected Works*, in 45 vols. (Moscow 1960–70)

CW	1:What the 'Friends of the People' Are and How They Fight the Social-Democrats	pp. 129–508
CW	2:The Tasks of the Russian Social-Democrats	323–54
CW	3:The Development of Capitalism in Russia	23–607
CW	4:What is to be Done?	347–530
CW	6:The Agrarian Programme of Russian Social-Democracy	107–50
CW	8:Social-Democracy and The Provisional Revolutionary Government	275–93
CW	9:Social-Democracy's Attitude towards the Peasant Movement	230–9
	Petty-bourgeois and Proletarian Socialism	438–46
CW	10:The Reorganisation of the Party	29–39
	A Tactical Platform for the Unity Congress of the RSDLP	147–64
CW	12:The Results of the Elections in the Workers' Curia in St Petersburg	86–92
CW	13:Preface to the Collection, *Twelve Years*	94–113
CW	14:Materialism and Empirio-Criticism	17–362
CW	16:The Historical Meaning of the Inner-Party Struggle in Russia	374–92
	Strike Statistics in Russia	393–422
	The Capitalist System of Modern Agriculture	423–46
CW	17:The Campaign for the Elections to the Fourth Duma	368–87
CW	21:The Draft Resolution Proposed by the Left Wing at Zimmerwald	345–8
	Several Theses	401–6
	On the Two Lines in the Revolution	415–20
CW	22:Imperialism, the Highest Stage of Capitalism	185–304
	The Junius Pamphlet	305–19
CW	23:Statistics and Sociology	271–7
CW	24:Letters on Tactics	42–54
CW	25:On Slogans	183–90
	The State and Revolution	381–493
CW	27:The Immediate Tasks of the Soviet Government	235–78
CW	28:Comrade Workers, Forward to the Last Decisive Fight	54–8
	Extraordinary Sixth All-Russia Congress of Soviets	135–64

References

The Proletarian Revolution and the Renegade Kautsky	227–325
Theses and Report on Bourgeois Democracy and the Dictatorship of the Proletariat (4 March 1919)	457–74
CW 30:Economics and Politics in the Era of the Dictatorship of the Proletariat	107–17
Draft (or Theses) of the R.C.P.'s Reply to the Letter of the Independent Social-Democratic Party of Germany	337–44
CW 31:*Kommunistmus*	165–7
Our Foreign and Domestic Position and Party Tasks	408–26
The Eighth All-Russian Congress of Soviets	461–534
CW 32:The Trade Unions, The Present Situation and Trotsky's Mistakes	19–42
Once Again on the Trade Unions, the Current Situation and the Mistakes of Trotsky and Bukharin	70–107
The Tax in Kind	329–65
CW 33:The Role and Functions of the Trade Unions under the New Economic Policy	184–96
Our Revolution	476–80
CW 38:Conspectus of Hegel's Book, *The Science of Logic*	85–238
On the Question of Dialectics	355–64

Levine, A. (1977). 'Balibar, on the Dictatorship of the Proletariat', in *Politics and Society*, vol.7.

Lewin, M. (1973). *Lenin's Last Struggle*, London: Wildwood House.

Liebman, M. (1975). *Leninism under Lenin*, London: Cape.

Lock, G. (1975). 'Introduction' to L. Althusser, *Essays in Self-Criticism*, London: New Left Books.

Lukacs, G. (1970). *Lenin* (1924), London: New Left Books.

Lukes, S. (1974a). *Power: A Radical View*, London: Macmillan.

Lukes, S. (1974b). 'Socialism and Equality', in L. Kolakowski and S. Hampshire (eds.), *The Socialist Idea*, London: Weidenfeld and Nicolson.

Luxemburg, R. (1961). 'Leninism or Marxism' (1904), in *The Russian Revolution and Marxism or Leninism*, Ann Arbor: University of Michigan Press.

Macintyre, A. (1971). *Against the Self-Images of the Age: Essays on Ideology and Philosophy*, London: Duckworth.

McClelland, J. C. (1978). 'Proletarianizing the Student Body: the Soviet Experience during the NEP', in *Past and Present* no. 80.

Mandel, E. (1969). *The Inconsistencies of State Capitalism*, London: International Marxist Group.

Mandel, E. (1974). 'Ten Theses on the Social and Economic Laws Governing the Society Transitional between Capitalism and Socialism', in *Critique*, no.3.

Mandel, E. (1978). *From Stalinism to Eurocommunism*, London: New Left Books.

Mao, Tse-Tung (1964). 'On Contradiction', in *Selected Works*, vol.1, Peking: Foreign Languages Press.

Marković, M. (1977). 'Stalinism and Marxism', in R. C. Tucker (ed.), *Stalinism*, New York: Norton.

Marsh, C. (1980). 'Underdevelopment and Compartmentalisation: Survey Research in Britain', paper delivered at British Sociological Association, Annual Conference.

References

Martov, L. (1911). in D. N. Ovsyaniko-Kulikovski (ed.), *Istoriya russkoy litera-tury XIXv*, Moscow.

Marx, K.

'The Class Struggles in France, 1848 to 1850', in Marx and Engels (1958), *SW* 1: 139–242.

'The Eighteenth Brumaire of Louis Napoleon', in Marx and Engels (1958), *SW* 1: 243–344.

'The Future Results of British Rule in India', in Marx and Engels (1958), *SW* 1: 345–51.

'Preface to *A Contribution to the Critique of Political Economy*', in Marx and Engels (1958), *SW* 1: 361–5.

'The Civil War in France', in Marx and Engels (1957), *SW* 1: 473–545.

'Critique of the Gotha Program', in Marx and Engels (1951), *SW* 2: 13–45.

Marx, K. (1968). *The German Ideology*, London: Laurence and Wishart.

Marx, K. and Engels, F. 'Manifesto of the Communist Party'; in Marx and Engels (1951), *SW* 1: 21–65.

Marx, K. and Engels, F. (1958). *Selected Works*, vol.1, Moscow: FLPH.

Marx, K and Engels, F. (1951). *Selected Works*, vol.2, Moscow: FLPH.

Maslov, P. (1967). *Sotsiologiya i Statistika*, Moscow.

Medvedev, R. (1971). *Let History Judge*, New York: Alfred Knopf.

Medvedev, R. (1979). *On Stalin and Stalinism*, Oxford: Oxford University Press.

Meyer, A. G. (1957). *Leninism*, New York: Praeger.

Miliband, R. (1975). 'Bettelheim and Soviet Experience', in *New Left Review*, no. 91.

Mommsen, W. J. (1974). *The Age of Bureaucracy*, Oxford: Basil Blackwell.

Morgan, G. A. (1967). 'Stalin on Revolution', in A. Simirenko (ed.), *Soviet Sociology*, London: Routledge.

Morgan, M. C. (1971). *Lenin*, London: Edward Arnold.

Navarro, V. (1978). *Class Struggle, the State and Medicine*, London: Martin Robertson.

Nisbet, R. A. (1965). *Émile Durkheim*, Englewood Cliffs, New Jersey: Prentice Hall.

Nove, A. (1961). 'The Soviet Model and Underdeveloped Countries', in *International Affairs*, vol.37, no.1.

Pannekoek, A. (1975). *Lenin as Philosopher*, London: Merlin.

Parekh, B. (1975). *The Concept of Socialism*, London: Croom Helm.

Parkin, F. (1979). *Marxism and Class Theory: a Bourgeois Critique*, London: Tavistock.

Parsons, T. (1951). *The Social System*, Glencoe, Ill.: The Free Press.

Parsons, T. (1959). 'General Theory in Sociology', in R. K. Merton et al., *Sociology Today*, vol.1, New York: Harper and Row.

Parsons, T. (1961). 'An Outline of the Social System', in T. Parsons, E. Shils et al., *Theories of Society*, vol.1, New York: Free Press.

Parsons, T. (1963). 'On the Concept of Political Power', in *Proceedings of the American Philosophical Society*, vol. 107, no. 3. Reprinted in R. Bendix and S. M. Lipset, *Class, Status and Power*, London: Routledge (1968).

Parsons, T. (1966a). *Societies: Evolutionary and Comparative Perspectives*, Englewood Cliffs, New Jersey: Prentice Hall.

References

Parsons, T. (1966b). 'Theory in the Humanities and Sociology', in *Daedalus*, vol.99, no.2.

Parsons, T. (1971). *The System of Modern Societies*, Englewood Cliffs, New Jersey: Prentice-Hall.

Parsons, T. and Bales, R. F. (1956). *Family, Socialisation and Interaction Process*, London: Routledge and Kegan Paul.

Parsons, T. and Shils, E. (1951). *Towards a General Theory of Action*, Cambridge, Mass.: Harvard University Press.

Pethybridge, R. (1974). *The Social Prelude to Stalinism*, London: Macmillan.

Piccone, P. (1977). 'On Infantile Diseases and Senile Diagnoses: the Case of Horton and Filsoufi', in *Telos*, no. 33.

Pipes, R. (1960). 'Russian Marxism and its Populist Background', in *Russian Review*, vol. 19, no.4.

Plamenatz, J. (1954). *German Marxism and Russian Communism*, London.

Pomper, P. (1978). 'Nečaev, Lenin and Stalin: The Psychology of Leadership', in *Jahrbücher fur Geschichte Osteuropas*, vol.26.

Poulantzas, N. (1973). *Political Power and Social Classes*, London: New Left Books.

Reisner, M. A. (1970). *Narodnoe prosveschchenie*, nos.6–7 (1919), p.142, cited in S. Fitzpatrick, *The Commissariat of Enlightenment*, Cambridge: Cambridge University Press.

Rocher, G. (1974). *Talcott Parsons and American Sociology*, London: Nelson.

Santamaria, U. and Manville, A. (1976). 'Lenin and the Problem of Transition', in *Telos*, no.27.

Scanlan, J. P. (1973). 'A Critique of the Engels – Soviet Version of Marxian Economic Determinism', in *Studies in Soviet Thought*, vol.13, nos. 1/2.

Schapiro, L. and Reddaway, P. (eds.). (1967). *Lenin: The Man, The Theorist, The Leader*, London: Pall Mall.

Serebrennikov, G. N. (1937). *The Position of Women in the USSR*, London: Gollancz.

Shanin, T. (ed.). (1971). *Peasants and Peasant Societies*, Harmondsworth: Penguin.

Shaw, M. (1975). *Marxism and Social Science*, London: Pluto Press.

Shirokov, M. (n.d.). *A Textbook of Marxist Philosophy*, translated by A. C. Moseley and J. Lewis, London: Gollancz.

Slaughter, C. (1978). 'Stalinism, Revisionism and the Dictatorship of the Proletariat', in *Labour Review*, vol.2, no.6.

Spours, K. (1978). 'Crisis in Soviet Ideology', in *Socialist Europe*, no.4.

Stalin, J. V. (1934a). *Foundations of Leninism*, Moscow: Co-operative Publishing Society of Foreign Workers in the USSR.

Stalin, J. V. (1934b). *Problems of Leninism*, Moscow: Co-operative Publishing Society of Foreign Workers in the USSR.

Stalin, J. V. (1973). 'Dialectical and Historical Materialism?' (first published 1938), in Franklin (1973).

Stedman-Jones, G. (1971). 'The Marxism of the Early Lukacs: An Evaluation', in *New Left Review*, no.70.

Sweezy, P. M. and Magdoff, H. (eds.). (1970). *Lenin Today*, New York and London: Monthly Review Press.

References

Sztompka, P. (1979). 'Marxism, Functionalism and Systems Analysis,' in J. J. Wiatr (ed.), *Polish Essays in the Methodology of the Social Sciences*. Dortrecht: D. Reidel.

Tellenback, S. (1978). *Prerequisites of Socialism: Industrial Society in a Comparative Perspective*, University of Lund: Department of Sociology.

Theen, R. H. W. (1973). *Lenin: Genesis and Development of a Revolutionary*, London: Quartet Books.

Thomson, G. (1971). *From Marx to Mao Tse-Tung*, London: China Policy Study Group.

Ticktin, H. H. (1973a). 'Towards a Political Economy of the USSR', in *Critique*, no. 1.

Ticktin, H. H. (1973b). 'Political Economy of the Soviet Intellectual', in *Critique*, no.2.

Ticktin, H. H. (1978). 'The Class Structure of the USSR and the Elite', in *Critique*, no.9.

Timasheff, N. S. (1946). *The Great Retreat*, New York: Dutton.

Timpanaro, S. (1975). *On Materialism*, London: New Left Books.

Tiryakian, E. A. (1970). 'Structural Sociology' in J. C. McKinney and E. A. Tiryakian (eds.), *Theoretical Sociology: Perspectives, and Development*, New York: Appleton-Century-Crofts.

Trotsky, L. (1958). *The Revolution Betrayed: The Soviet Union, what it is and where it is going* (written 1936), New York: Pioneer Publishers.

Trotsky, L. (1962). *Permanent Revolution* (first published in Russian, 1930) and *Results and Prospects* (first published in Russian, 1919), London: New Park Publications.

Trotsky, L. (1967). *The Russian Revolution*, vol.1, London: Sphere Books.

Trotsky, L. (1968). *The Class Nature of the Soviet State* and *The Question of the Thermidor and Bonapartism*, London: New Park.

Trotsky, L. (1970). 'The 21st Anniversary', in *The Writings of Leon Trotsky (1937–38)*, New York: Pathfinder Press.

Trotsky, L. (1972). *The Young Lenin*, Newton Abbot: David and Charles.

Tucker, R. C. (1977a). 'Some Questions on the Scholarly Agenda', in Tucker (1977b).

Tucker, R. C. (1977b). *Stalinism: Essays in Historical Interpretation*, New York: W. W. Norton.

Ulam, A. (1955). 'The Historical Role of Marxism and the Soviet System', in *World Politics*, vol. 8, no. 1.

Utechin, S. V. (1960). 'Who Taught Lenin', in *Twentieth Century*, vol. CLXVIII.

Ward, B. (1962). *The Rich Nations and the Poor Nations*, New York: W. W. Norton.

Weber, M. (1947). *The Theory of Social and Economic Organization*, Chicago: Free Press.

White, S. (1979). *Political Culture and Soviet Politics*, London: Macmillan.

Wolf, C. P. (1976). 'The Structure of Societal Revolutions', in Zollschan and Hirsch (1976).

Wright, E. O. (1978). *Class, Crisis and the State*, London: New Left Books.

Zollschan, G. K. and Hirsch, W. (eds.). (1976). *Social Change. Explorations, Diagnoses and Conjectures*, New York: John Wiley.

Zollschan, G. K. and Hirsch, W. (eds.). (1964). *Explorations in Social Change*, Boston: Houghton Mifflin.

Index

Index

Index